# A HISTORY OF THE
# JEWISH FAITH

Neron lempereur lors estant en achaye ou il se occupoit aux chanteries et melodies turgiques sachant que ses affaires et besongnes se portoient inutilement z non prosperement en iudee fut tantost spris et esmeu de desplaisir

pour et araimete Car combien que par dehors et en appert il simulast et demonstrast faintement son orgueil Si estoit il indigne desplaisant et trouble et disoit que ces desobeissaniz rebellions et aduersitez contre la chose publicque de romme estoient plus aduenues par la negligence

# A HISTORY OF THE
# JEWISH FAITH

## THE DEVELOPMENT OF JUDAISM FROM ANCIENT TIMES
## TO THE MODERN DAY, SHOWN IN OVER 190 PICTURES

### PROFESSOR DAN COHN-SHERBOK

southwater

*Above A rabbinical debate, 1888.*

*Above The ancient city of Jerusalem.*

*Above The Western Wall in Jerusalem.*

This edition is published by Southwater, an imprint of Anness Publishing Ltd, 108 Great Russell Street, London WC1B 3NA; info@anness.com

www.southwaterbooks.com; www.annesspublishing.com; twitter: @Anness_Books

Anness Publishing has a new picture agency outlet for images for publishing, promotions or advertising. Please visit our website www.practicalpictures.com for more information.

© Anness Publishing Ltd 2015

A CIP catalogue record for this book is available from the British Library.

Publisher: Joanna Lorenz
Senior Editor: Felicity Forster
Maps: Anthony Duke
Designer: Nigel Partridge
Production Controller: Rosanna Anness

Previously published as part of a larger volume, *The Illustrated Guide to Judaism*

PUBLISHER'S NOTE
Although the information in this book is believed to be accurate and true at the time of going to press, neither the authors nor the publisher can accept any legal responsibility or liability for any errors or omissions that may have been made.

*p1 Strictly Orthodox Jews pray for peace in the Lebanon at the grave of mystic Isaac Luria in Safed, Israel.*
*p2 Jewish historian Flavius Josephus, who described the Hasmonean revolt, is brought before Titus, Roman commander in Judea during the Jewish revolt 66CE.*
*p3 A Hasidic Jew holds the lulav and etrog in a sukkah built for Sukkot in Williamsburg, New York.*

PICTURE ACKNOWLEDGEMENTS
akg-images: 14b, 17b, 18t, 19bl, 20b, 24br, 25b, 31b, 34b, 48b, 54t, 55t, 56b, 74b, 80t, 81b, 85b; Bible Land Pictures 33bl&br, 49tr; Bildarchiv Pisarek 78t, 94t; British Library 8; Electa 29b; Erich Lessing 15bl, 24bl, 30bl, 38bl, 52t, 55b, 80b; Horizons 92b; Israel Images 7t, 19br, 32b, 33t, 38br, 39, 46t, 50b, 60t, 61bl; János Kalmár 41; Jürgen Raible 12; North Wind Picture Archives 18b; Suzanne Held 50t, 79t&b.
Alamy: © john norman 53b; © 19th era 2, 57t; © Arcaid 59; © Art Directors & TRIP 66b; © david sanger photography 91tl; © Eddie Gerald 73t; © Eitan Simanor 75b; © Hanan Isachar 53t; © INTERFOTO 86t; © J. Wolanczyk 57b; © Jean Dominique Dallet 46b; © Jeff Morgan 06, 71b; © Jim West 71t; © Lebrecht Music and Arts Photo Library 25t, 43tr, 52b; © moris kushelevitch 7b; © Nathan Benn 95b; © PhotoStock-Israel 88t; © Richard Levine 75tl; © The Art Gallery Collection 30t; © www.BibleLandPictures.com 19t, 27b, 28t, 30br, 45b, 61t.
The Art Archive: American Colony Photographers/NGS Image Collection, 32t; Bibliothèque Mazarine Paris/CCI, 26bl; Bibliothèque Municipale Valenciennes/Gianni Dagli Orti 26br; Bibliothèque Universitaire de Mèdecine, Montpellier/Gianni Dagli Orti 44t; Bodleian Library Oxford, 40; British Library 42t, 43tl; Castello della Manta Piemonte/Collection Dagli Orti 37t; CCI 6bl; Culver Pictures 54b; Eileen Tweedy 47br; Hunt Add E (R)/Bodleian Library Oxford 47bl; Laud. Or.234 fol. 83V/Bodleian Library Oxford 49tl; National Museum of Bosnia Herzegovina,

Sarajevo 14t; Palatine Library Parma/Gianni Dagli Orti 26t; Palazzo Leoni-Montanari Vicenza/Gianni Dagli Orti 45t; San Apollinare Nuovo Ravenna/Collection Dagli Orti 36b; University Library Istanbul/Gianni Dagli Ort 27t, 44b.
Bridgeman Images: 5r, 6t, 9, 35b, 38t, 47t, 56t, 94b; Photo © Bonhams, London, UK 4l, 78b; © British Library Board. All Rights Reserved 5l, 31t; Bibliotheque Nationale, Paris, France 17t; DaTo Images 76, 93; Gift of James A. de Rothschild, London 10, 42b; Giraudon 15t, 35tl; Photo © Zev Radovan 22, 24t, 36t, 37br.
Corbis: 4m, 23, 63tl, 70b; © Andrew Aitchison/In Pictures 62t; © Aristide Economopoulos/Star Ledger, 69t; © Bettmann 21tl, 60b, 64b, 65, 86tr&bl; © Bojan Brecelj 43b; © Catherine Karnow 89b; © Catherine Ledner 82t; © Ed Kashi 88b; © Gianni Dagli Orti 28bl; © Hanan Isachar/JAI 63b; © Heritage Images 2, 34t; © Hulton-Deutsch Collection 21tr; © Jacques Loew/Kipa 86br; © Jason Horowitz 61br; © Jim Hollander/epa 4r, 77; © John Stanmeyer/VII 95t; © Jonathan Ernst/Reuters 72t; © Lebrecht Music & Arts 84b; © Leland Bobbé 5m, 64t; © Les Stone/Sygma 83t&b; © Lucy Nicholson/Reuters, 89t; © Mark Peterson 63tr; © Michael Nicholson 29t; © MIRIAM ALSTER/epa 87; © Nathan Benn/Ottochrome 3, 62b; © Neal Preston 91b; © Oscar White 85tl; © Richard T. Nowitz 6br, 13, 51b, 82b; © Shai Ginott 37bl; © STR/Reuters 1, 51t; © Ted Spiegel 58, 67b; ©YANNIS BEHRAKIS/Reuters 92t; Image © Bettmann 66t; 67t, 81tl&tr.
Photo12: 20t, 35tr; Ann Ronan Picture Library 15br, 16t; Oronoz 48t.
Rex Features: Alinari 75tr; Everett Collection 84t.
Rodger Kamenetz: © Rodger Kamenetz 72b, 73b, 90b; John Bigelow Taylor/courtesy of the International Campaign for Tibet 91tr.
Eisenstein Reconstructionist Archives, Reconstructionist Rabbinical College, Wyncote, PA: 68t, bl&r, 69b.
Society for Humanistic Judaism (www.shj.org; www.hujews.org): 70t.

# CONTENTS

*Below Menelaus bribing Antiochus IV.*

*Below Traditional foods eaten at Passover.*

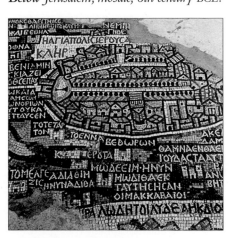

*Below Jerusalem, mosaic, 6th century BCE.*

# INTRODUCTION

IS JUDAISM A UNIFIED RELIGIOUS TRADITION, OR HAVE VARIETIES OF JUDAISM EXISTED THROUGH THE CENTURIES? DO ALL JEWS SUBSCRIBE TO THE SAME BELIEFS? OR DO THEY ALL OBSERVE THE SAME RITUALS?

These are the central questions that this volume seeks to explore. Divided into four major sections – Ancient Judaism, Rabbinic Judaism, Modern Judaism and Untraditional Judaism – this work surveys the wide variety of forms of the Jewish tradition through the centuries from biblical times to the present. Throughout it draws heavily on images of the Jew as portrayed in the Western artistic tradition.

## ANCIENT JUDAISM
The history of the Jewish people is grounded in Scripture. According to the Hebrew Bible, God chose Abraham as the founder of the Jewish nation. According to the Book of Genesis, he was prepared to sacrifice his son, Isaac, out of obedience to God. The biblical account continues with the patriarchal narratives, and eventually the Exodus from Egypt. Later, following the

*Below A French postcard for Jewish New Year showing worshippers in prayer shawls, c. 1920.*

conquest of Canaanites, the ancient Israelites settled in the land, established the Temple as their centre of worship, and were ruled over by a succession of kings in the Northern and Southern Kingdoms. In the 8th century BCE the Northern Kingdom (Israel) was conquered by the Assyrians; two centuries later the Babylonians invaded the Southern Kingdom (Judah), and led Jewish captives back to Babylonia. Later in the 6th century BCE, the Persians conquered the Babylonians and allowed Jews to return to their native land. During the ensuing Hellenistic period, the Pharisees, Sadducees and Essenes competed with one another for religious dominance.

## RABBINIC JUDAISM
Following a Jewish rebellion against the Romans in the 1st century CE, Jerusalem was devastated and the Temple destroyed. In the years that followed the Pharisees dominated Jewish life. During this period, rabbinic scholars engaged in debate about the interpretation of biblical

*Above Dutch artist Rembrandt's painting of* Moses with the Ten Commandments, *1659.*

law and expounded the meaning of the narrative sections of Scripture. The most important scholar of the early rabbinic period was Yehuda Ha-Nasi, the head of the Sanhedrin, whose main achievement was the composition of the Mishnah, a compendium of the oral law. This volume consisted of the discussions and rulings of sages whose teachings

*Below A modern synagogue in Teaneck, New Jersey, USA, with a beautiful stained-glass window.*

*Above Prayer with Torah scroll at the Western Wall, Jerusalem, on the 9th of Av, the anniversary of the destruction of both the First and Second Temples.*

had been transmitted orally. Alongside the Mishnah, rabbinic scholars also contributed to a variety of midrashim (collections of interpretations of the Biblical text). In later centuries, the rabbis composed mystical Kabbalistic treatises as well as philosophical studies dealing with God's nature and activity. Alongside this efflorescence of Jewish scholarship, a number of sects – the Karaites, Shabbateans and the Frankists – propounded different and opposing views of the Jewish tradition.

## MODERN JUDAISM

In modern times Judaism has splintered into a wide range of religious groups espousing varied interpretations of the tradition. Strictly Orthodox Jews, including the Hasidim, steadfastly adhere to the belief that God revealed both the Written and the Oral Torah. For these Jews, the Code of Jewish Law serves as the framework for Jewish life. In the early 19th century the Reform movement emerged as an alternative form of Judaism. In the view of the early Reformers, the

Jewish heritage must be modified to suit the modern temperament. In a series of synods held in Europe and the United States, Reform rabbis advocated the retention of only those laws which were spiritually relevant for contemporary times. In addition, they rejected those traditional beliefs which in their view had lost their relevance for contemporary Jewry. Later, Conservative Jews separated themselves from the Orthodox, but were less radical in their approach than the Reformers. Subsequently, other movements – Reconstructionist Judaism, Humanistic Judaism and Jewish Renewal – offered alternative approaches to the Jewish tradition.

## UNTRADITIONAL JUDAISM

Alongside the major Jewish denominations, other groups have espoused a wide range of interpretations of the Jewish heritage. At the end of the 19th century, secular Zionists championed the idea of a Jewish homeland in Palestine. In their view,

Jews will never be secure in the Diaspora; what is needed instead is for Jews to live in their ancient homeland. Only in this way will they free themselves from persecution and destruction. In time, these secular Zionists were joined by religious Zionists who maintained that a Jewish return to Zion is a precondition of messianic redemption. Alongside this development, modern Kabbalists have fostered a mystical approach to Jewish life based on the study of mystical texts. Other Jews have joined a wide variety of groups, including the Jewish Left, Jewish feminists, Jewish vegetarians, Jewish Buddhists and Jewish environmentalists. In all these cases, Jewish values are of central importance despite the varying understanding of Jewish history.

*Below Prayer at the tomb in Meron, Israel, of Rabbi Simeon ben Yohai, traditionally the author of the Zohar, the most important medieval text of Kabbalistic Judaism.*

# TIMELINE

THIS IS A CHRONOLOGICAL TIMELINE OF THE JEWISH PEOPLE. IT LISTS SOME OF THE MAJOR EVENTS IN JUDAISM'S CULTURALLY AND POLITICALLY DIVERSE HISTORY OVER THOUSANDS OF YEARS.

### 2000–700BCE

*c.*2000–1700BCE According to tradition, the age of the Patriarchs begins with Abraham. The Israelites leave Canaan for Egypt when famine strikes.

*c.*1700BCE Joseph is sold into slavery. He later welcomes his family to Egypt.

*c.* 1700–1300BCE Enslavement of the Israelites.

*c.*1300–1200BCE Moses leads the Israelites from Egypt.

*c.*1280BCE Torah, including the Ten Commandments, received by Moses at Mount Sinai.

*c.*1240BCE The Israelites conquer Canaan under Joshua.

*c.*1200–1000BCE Time of Judges.

1050BCE Philistines vanquish Shiloh and win the Ark of the Covenant. The time of Samuel, prophet and last judge.

1020BCE Saul is first King of the United Kingdom of Israel and Judah; rules until 1007BCE.

*c.*1004–965BCE King David crowned in Bethlehem. He makes Jerusalem his new capital and installs Ark of the Covenant.

*c.*965–928BCE Solomon is crowned. The Kingdom expands. First Temple is built.

*c.*928BCE Rehoboam is king. Kingdom splits into Judah and Israel (under Jeroboam).

918BCE Shishak of Egypt invades Israel.

*c.*900–800BCE Time of prophet Elijah.

727–698BCE King Hezekiah of Judah introduces major religious reforms.

722BCE Assyrians take over Israel. Ten Tribes disperse. Time of the prophet Isaiah.

### 700–100BCE

639–609BCE King Josiah makes religious reforms in Judah. Dies at Battle of Megiddo (Armageddon) fighting Assyrian and Egyptian forces.

586BCE Babylonians conquer Judah and destroy Jerusalem and the Temple. Most Jews are exiled to Babylon (the first Diaspora).

*c.*580BCE Jews establish colony on the Nile island of Elephantine, Egypt.

538–445BCE Under King Cyrus, the Persians defeat the Babylonians. Jews return to Israel, led by Zerubbabel and scribes Ezra and Nehemiah. Temple and city walls rebuilt in Jerusalem. Canonization of the Torah.

536–142BCE Persian and Hellenistic periods.

*c.*500–400BCE Canonization of Book of Prophets. Presumed period of Queen Esther and the Purim saga in Persia. Elephantine Temple destroyed in Egypt.

347BCE Time of the Great Assembly, end of kingship.

332BCE Land conquered by Alexander the Great; Hellenistic rule.

285–244BCE 72 Jewish sages translate Torah into Greek; called the Septuagint.

219–217BCE Rival Hellenistic dynasties fight for control of Israel. Seleucids finally displace Ptolemaids in 198BCE.

166–160BCE Maccabean (Hasmonean) revolt.

142–129BCE Jewish autonomy under Hasmoneans. In Jerusalem the zugot, or pairs of sages, acquire more power.

138BCE The rededication of the Second Temple. Foundation of Dead Sea Jewish sect at Qumran.

129–63BCE Jewish independence under Hasmonean monarchy.

*Above 'We were slaves in Egypt', from a 14th-century Spanish illumination.*

### 100BCE–300CE

63BCE Romans invade Israel. Jerusalem captured by Pompey who names Judea a Roman vassal.

37BCE–4CE Herod the Great rules Israel. Temple in Jerusalem refurbished. Sanhedrin acts as Jewish legislature and judicial council.

*c.*30BCE–30CE Time of rabbis Hillel and Shammai.

6CE Judea becomes Roman province with capital at Caesarea.

*c.*20–36CE Ministry of Jesus of Nazareth.

30–100CE The birth of Christianity.

66–73CE The Great Revolt of Jews against Rome.

70CE Jerusalem conquered by Romans. Second Temple destroyed.

70–200CE Period of the tannaim, sages who organized the Jewish oral law.

115–117CE Jewish revolt against Rome.

131CE Hadrian renames Jerusalem Aelia Capitolina and forbids Jews to enter.

132–135CE Rebellion of Bar Kochba against Rome and Hadrian. Rome renames Judea 'Syria Palestina'.

*c.*210CE Mishnah (standardization of the Jewish oral law) compiled by Rabbi Yehuda Ha-Nasi. By now, Ketuvim (Writings) are canonized.

212CE Jews accepted as Roman citizens.

245CE Dura-Europos synagogue built in northern Syria.

### 300–600CE

220–500CE Period of the amoraim, the sages of the Talmud. The main redaction of Talmud Bavli (Babylonian Talmud) is completed by 475CE.

305CE Council of Elvira in Spain forbids Christians to socialize with Jews.

313–37CE Emperor Constantine converts Roman Empire to Christianity. The Empire is split into two, and the Eastern, or Byzantine Empire, becomes more powerful. Jews come under Byzantine rule in 330.

313–636CE Byzantine rule.

351CE A Jewish revolt in Galilee directed against Gallus Caesar is soon crushed.

361–3CE The last pagan Roman emperor, Julian, allows Jews to return to Jerusalem and rebuild the Temple. The project lapses when he dies and his successor Jovian re-establishes Christianity as the imperial religion.

c.390CE Mishnah commentary (written form of oral traditions) completed. Hillel II formulates Jewish calendar.

400–50CE Redaction of Talmud Yerushalmi (Talmud of Jerusalem).

425CE Jerusalem's Jewish patriarchate is abolished.

438CE The Empress Eudocia removes the ban on Jews praying at the Temple site.

489CE Theodoric, King of the Ostrogoths, conquers Italy and protects the Jews.

502CE Mar Zutra II establishes a Jewish state in Babylon.

525–29CE End of Himyar Jewish Kingdom in southern Arabia. Byzantine Emperor Justinian I issues anti-Jewish legislation.

550–700CE Period of the savoraim, sages in Persia who finalized the Talmud.

556CE Jews and Samaritans revolt against Byzantines. Midrashic literature and liturgical poetry developed.

### 600–750CE

7th century CE Foundation of the Khazar kingdom in Caucasus, southern Russia. Birth of Islam. The domination of Islam in the Arabian Peninsula results in the destruction of most Jewish communities there. Jews in the far southern realm of Yemen are mostly unaffected.

608–10CE Jews riot in Antioch, Syria, killing the Christians. This facilitates the entrance of Persian troops. Anti-Jewish pogroms break out from Syria to Asia Minor.

613CE, Jews gain autonomy in Jerusalem after a Persian-backed revolt.

613–14CE Persian invasion of Palestine brings the Byzantine period to an end.

629CE Byzantines retake Palestine and kill many Jews; survivors flee.

632CE Death of Islamic Prophet Mohammed.

636–1099CE Arab rule.

638CE Islamic and Arab conquest of Jerusalem. Arabs permit some Jews to return to Jerusalem, including immigrants from Babylon and refugees from Arabia.

640–2CE Arabs conquer Egypt.

691CE Dome of the Rock built by Caliph Abd el-Malik on site of the First and Second Temples in Jerusalem.

694–711CE The Visigoths outlaw Judaism.

700–1250CE Period of the Gaonim, presidents of the rabbinical colleges in Sura and Pumbedita, Babylon. New Jewish academies arise in Kairouan, Tunisia, and Fez, Morocco.

711CE Muslim armies invade and within a few years occupy most of Spain.

c.740CE Khazar Khanate royals and many Khazars convert to Judaism.

750–950CE Heyday of the Masoretes in Tiberias, Palestine, who codified Torah annotations, vocalizations and grammar.

### 750–1050CE

760CE The Karaites reject the authority of the oral law, and split off from rabbinic Judaism.

763–809CE Reign of Haran al Rashid (Persia), fifth Abbasid Caliph.

807CE Haran al Rashid forces Jews to wear a yellow badge and Christians to wear a blue badge.

808CE Fez (Morocco) becomes the capital of the Shiite dynasty under Idris II who allows Jews to live in their own quarter in return for an annual tax.

809–13CE Civil war in Persia.

900–1090CE The Golden age of Jewish culture in Spain.

912CE Abd-ar-Rahman III becomes Caliph of Spain.

940CE In Iraq, Saadia Gaon compiles his siddur (Jewish prayer book).

953CE Jewish historical narrative, Josippon, written in southern Italy.

960–1028CE Rabbenu Gershom of Germany, first great Ashkenazi sage, bans bigamy.

1013–73 Life of Rabbi Yitzhak Alfassi, who wrote the *Rif*, an important work of Jewish law.

1040–1105 Time of Rashi of France, Rabbi Shlomo Yitzhaki, who writes commentaries on almost the entire Tanakh (Hebrew Bible) and Talmud.

*Below A 5th-century CE mosaic map from Madaba, showing Jerusalem.*

### 1050–1250

1066 Jews enter England in the wake of the Norman invasion under William the Conqueror.

1090 Granada is conquered by the Muslim Berber Almoravides, ending the period of tolerance. Jews flee to Toledo.

1095–1291 Christian Crusades begin, sparking warfare with Islam in Palestine. Thousands of Jews are killed in Europe and in the Middle East.

1099 Crusaders temporarily capture Jerusalem.

1100–1275 Time of the tosafot, medieval talmudic commentators on the Torah carrying on Rashi's work.

1107 Moroccan Almoravid ruler Yoseph Ibn Tashfin expels Moroccan Jews who do not convert to Islam.

1135–1204 Rabbi Moses ben Maimon, aka Maimonides, is the leading rabbi of Sephardic Jewry. He writes the *Mishneh Torah* and the *Guide for the Perplexed*.

1141 Yehuda Halevi (1075–1141) issues a call for Jews to emigrate to Palestine.

1144 First Blood Libel, in Norwich, England. The trend spreads to Europe.

1179 Third Lateran Council in Vatican establishes Jewish-Christian relations.

1187 Arab leader Saladin (*c*.1138–1193) takes Jerusalem and most of Palestine; many Jews arrive.

1200–1300 Zenith of the German Jewish Hasidei Ashkenaz pietist movement.

1240 Paris Disputation. Monks publicly burn the Talmud.

1244–1500 Successive conquest of Palestine by Mongols and Egyptian Muslims. Many Jews die or leave.

1249 Pope Innocent IV in Italy forbids Christians to make false blood libels against Jews.

### 1250–1480

1250–1300 The time of Moses de Leon of Spain, reputed author of the Zohar. Modern form of Kabbalah (esoteric Jewish mysticism) begins.

1250–1516 Mamluk rule.

1250–1550 Period of the Rishonim, the rabbinic sages who wrote commentaries on the Torah and Talmud and law codes.

1263 The Great Disputation of Barcelona, where Nahmanides (Ramban) defends the Talmud against Christian accusations.

1267 Nahmanides settles in Jerusalem and builds the Ramban Synagogue.

1270–1343 Rabbi Jacob ben Asher of Spain writes the *Arba'ah Turim* (Four Rows of Jewish Law).

1290 Jews are expelled from England by Edward I by the Statute of Jewry.

1290–1301 Mamluk rulers allow attacks on churches and synagogues, and segregate Jews and Christians from Muslims.

1300 Time of Rabbi Levi ben Gershom (1288–1344), also known as Gersonides, a French philosopher.

1306–94 Jews are repeatedly expelled from France and readmitted. Last expulsion lasts 150 years.

1343 Persecuted in west Europe, Jews are invited to Poland by Casimir the Great.

1348–50 The Plague kills 30 to 60 per cent of Europe's people, and some blame Jews.

1391 Massacres in Spain; Jewish refugees find sanctuary in Algeria.

1415 Pope Benedict XII orders censorship of Talmud.

1458 Jews welcome Ottoman Turks who conquer Byzantine Constantinople.

1475 First Hebrew book printed, in Italy, Ben Asher's *Arba'ah Turim*.

1478 The Spanish Inquisition begins.

### 1480–1550

1486 First Jewish prayer book published in Italy.

1487 Portugal's first printed book is a Pentateuch in Hebrew.

1488–1575 Life of Joseph Caro, born in Spain, who in later years wrote the *Shulkhan Arukh*, the codification of halakhic law and talmudic rulings.

1492 The Alhambra Decree – 200,000 Jews are expelled from Spain. Ottoman Sultan Bayezid II sends ships to bring Jews to safety in his empire. Many Jews survive as conversos (converts) or marranos, or flee. Columbus discovers America.

1493 Jews are expelled from Sicily.

1495 Jews expelled from Lithuania.

1497 Jews are forced to convert or leave Portugal.

1501 King Alexander of Poland readmits Jews to the Grand Duchy of Lithuania.

1516 Ghetto of Venice established.

1517 Martin Luther starts the Protestant Reformation.

1517–1917 Ottoman rule in Palestine.

1525–72 Rabbi Moses Isserles (The Rama) of Cracow writes an extensive gloss to the *Shulkhan Arukh* for Ashkenazi Jewry.

1525–1609 Life of Rabbi Judah Loew ben Betzalel, called Maharal of Prague.

1534 First Yiddish book published, in Poland.

1547 First Hebrew Jewish printing house in Lublin, Poland.

*Below The 15th-century* Rothschild Miscellany *details all of Jewish life.*

## 1550–1720

1534–70 Life of Isaac Luria, who founded the new school of Kabbalists.

1550 Moses ben Jacob Cordovero founds a Kabbalah academy in Safed.

1564 First printed version of Joseph Caro's Code of Jewish law published.

1567 First Jewish university yeshiva founded in Poland.

1577 Hebrew printing press established in Safed, the first of any kind in Asia.

1580–1764 First session of the Council of Four Lands (Va'ad Arba' Aratzot) in Lublin, Poland. Seventy delegates from local Jewish kehillot meet to discuss issues important to the Jewish community.

1626–76 Time of false Messiah Shabbetai Tzvi of Smyrna, Turkey.

1648–55 Ukrainian Cossack Bogdan Chmielnicki leads a massacre of Polish gentry and Jewry that leaves an estimated 130,000 dead. The total decrease in the number of Jews is estimated at 100,000.

1654 The first Jews go to North America.

1655 Jews are readmitted to England.

1675 The world's first Jewish newspaper is printed in Amsterdam.

1700 Rabbi Yehuda He-Hasid makes aliyah (immigrates) to Palestine with hundreds of followers. He dies suddenly.

1700–60 Life of Israel ben Eliezer, known as the Ba'al Shem Tov, who founded Hasidic Judaism in eastern Poland.

1701 Foundation of Bevis Marks Synagogue, London, the oldest synagogue in the United Kingdom still in use.

1720 Unpaid Arab creditors burn the unfinished synagogue built by immigrants of Rabbi Yehuda and expel all Ashkenazi Jews from Jerusalem.

1720–97 Time of Rabbi Elijah of Vilna, the Vilna Gaon.

## 1720–1800s

1729–86 Moses Mendelssohn and the Haskalah (Enlightenment) movement.

1740 Ottomans invite Rabbi Haim Abulafia (1660–1744) to rebuild Tiberias.

1740–50 Mass immigration to Palestine under messianic predictions.

1747 Rabbi Abraham Gershon of Kitov is the first immigrant of the Hasidic Aliyah.

1759 Time of Jacob Frank (who claimed to be the reincarnation of Shabbetai Tzvi and King David).

1772–95 Partitions of Poland between Russia, Kingdom of Prussia and Austria where most Jews live. Old Jewish privileges are renounced.

1775–81 American Revolution, which guaranteed the freedom of religion.

1789 The French Revolution leads France in 1791 to grant full citizen rights to Jews, under certain conditions.

1790 In the USA, George Washington writes to the Jews of Rhode Island that he wants a country 'which gives bigotry no sanction ... persecution no assistance'.

1791 Emancipation of Jews begins in Europe. Russia creates the Pale of Settlement.

1799 Failed attempt by the French to seize Acre in Palestine.

1800–1900 The Golden Age of Yiddish literature, the revival of Hebrew as a spoken language, and the revival of Hebrew literature. First major Yiddish theatre founded in Romania in 1876.

1810 Reform Movement in Germany opens first synagogue in Seesen.

1820–60 The development of Orthodox Judaism, in response to Reform Judaism, the European emancipation and Enlightenment movements; it is characterized by strict adherence to halakha (Jewish religious law).

*Above The Portuguese Sephardic Synagogue in Amsterdam, built 1671.*

## 1800s–1870

Mid-1800s Rabbi Israel Salanter develops the Mussar Movement. Positive-Historical Judaism, later known as Conservative Judaism, is developed.

1841 David Levy Yulee of Florida is the first Jew elected to Congress. The *Jewish Chronicle* is first printed in the UK.

1851 Norway allows Jews to enter the country. They are emancipated in 1891.

1858 Jews emancipated in England.

1860 Alliance Israélite Universelle is founded in Paris with the goal to protect Jewish rights as citizens.

1860–1943 Time of Henrietta Szold, founder of Hadassah.

1861 The Zion Society is formed in Frankfurt am Main, Germany. The first Haskalah Russian journal, *Razsvet*, is founded.

1862 Jews are given equal rights in Russia's Congress Kingdom of Poland. Moses Hess writes his proto-Zionist tract, *Rome and Jerusalem*.

1867 Jews emancipated in Hungary.

1868 Converted Jew Benjamin Disraeli becomes Prime Minister of the United Kingdom.

1870–90 Russian Zionist group Hovevei Zion (Lovers of Zion) and Bilu (est. 1882) set up a series of Jewish settlements in Israel, financially aided by Baron Edmond James de Rothschild. Eliezer Ben-Yehuda revives Hebrew as a spoken modern language.

*Above Memorial in Berlin for the murdered Jews of Europe.*

## 1870–1914

1870-1 Jews are emancipated in Italy and then Germany.

1875 Reform Judaism's Hebrew Union College is founded in Cincinnati, USA.

1877 New Hampshire becomes the last US state to give Jews equal rights.

1881–4, 1903–6, 1918–20 Three waves of pogroms kill thousands of Jews in Russia and Ukraine.

1882–1903 First Aliyah (large-scale immigration) to Israel, mainly from Russia.

1887 Conservative Jewish movement founded in America.

1890 The term 'Zionism' is coined by Nathan Birnbaum.

1897 Theodor Herzl writes *Der Judenstaat* (The Jewish State). The Bund (General Jewish Labor Union) is formed in Russia. The first Zionist Congress meets in Switzerland; the Zionist Organization founded.

1902 The Jewish Theological Seminary becomes the flagship of Conservative Judaism. Theodor Herzl publishes utopian Zionist novel *Altneuland*.

1903 The Kishinev Pogrom is caused by accusations that Jews practise cannibalism.

1904–14 The Second Aliyah, mainly from Russia and Poland.

1905 Russian Revolution, accompanied by pogroms.

1909 The first kibbutz and Tel Aviv are founded.

## 1914–33

1914 American Jewish Joint Distribution Committee founded.

1915 Yeshiva College and Rabbinical Seminary is established in New York.

1917 British military governance over Palestine begins after Allenby's troops defeat Ottoman Turks. Balfour Declaration gives official British support for 'the establishment in Palestine of a national home for the Jewish people'. The Pale of Settlement in Russia is abolished, and Jews get equal rights. Russian civil war leads to more than 2,000 pogroms.

1918–48 British Rule of Palestine.

1919–23 Third Aliyah, mainly from Russia.

1920 Histadrut (Jewish labour federation) and Haganah (Jewish defence organization) are founded in Israel. Vaad Leumi (National Council) is set up by the Jewish community. Britain receives the League of Nations' British Mandate of Palestine.

1921 British military administration of the Mandate is replaced by civilian rule. Britain proclaims that all Palestine east of the Jordan River is closed to Jewish settlement, but not to Arab settlement. Polish-Soviet peace treaty in Riga. First moshav (cooperative village), Nahalal, founded in Israel.

1922 Transjordan set up on three-quarters of Palestine. Jewish Agency is established. Establishment of the Jewish Institute of Religion in New York. Reconstructionist movement is established.

1923 Britain awards Golan Heights to Syria. Arab immigration is allowed; Jewish immigration is not.

1924–32 Fourth Aliyah, mainly from Poland.

1929 Major Arab riots in Palestine.

1931 Etzel (Irgun) 'revisionist' Jewish underground organization, founded.

## 1933–67

1933 Hitler takes over Germany and begins imposing race laws against Jews.

1933–9 Fifth Aliyah, mainly from Germany.

1936 World Jewish Congress founded.

1938 9-10 November: Kristallnacht (Night of Glass) – Nazi violence against Jews.

1939 The British government announces a limit of 75,000 on future Jewish immigration to Palestine.

1939–45 World War II. Holocaust.

1945–8 Post-Holocaust refugee crisis.

1946–8 The struggle for the creation of a Jewish state in Palestine is resumed by Haganah, Irgun and Lehi militants.

1947 Discovery of Dead Sea Scrolls.

1947 29 November: The United Nations approves creation of a Jewish State and an Arab State in Palestine. Violence erupts between Jews and Arabs.

1948 14 May: The State of Israel declares independence.

1948 15 May: Arab–Israeli War.

1948–9 War of Independence. Almost 250,000 Holocaust survivors make their way to Israel. 'Operation Magic Carpet' brings Yemenite Jews to Israel.

1948–54 Mass immigration to Israel.

1952 Prague trials revive anti-Semitic fears in Communist eastern bloc.

1953 Establishment of Yad Vashem Holocaust Memorial in Israel.

1956 The Suez War.

1962–5 Jewish–Christian relations are revolutionized by Vatican II.

1964 Palestine Liberation Organization (PLO) founded.

1966 Shmuel Yosef Agnon (1888–1970) becomes the first Hebrew writer to win the Nobel Prize in literature; jointly with German Jewish author Nelly Sachs.

### 1967–80

1967 5–11 June: Six Day War fought between Jewish Israel and Arab Egypt, Syria and Jordan. Israel gains control of East Jerusalem, West Bank, Sinai Peninsula and Golan Heights.

1967 1 September: Arab Leaders meet in Khartoum: – the Three Nos of Khartoum: No recognition of Israel; No negotiations with Israel; No peace with Israel. UN 242 offers 'land for peace' formula and underpins most future peace plans.

1968–70 Egypt's War of Attrition against Israel, to recapture the Sinai held by Israel since the Six Day War. Jewish settlers occupy houses in Hebron, amid more than 100,000 Palestinians.

1972 After a brief window in 1971, Soviets clamp down on 'refusenik' Jews wishing to leave the USSR. Palestinian terrorists kill Israeli athletes at Munich Olympics.

1973 6–24 October: Yom Kippur War. Israel surprised by Egyptian–Syrian attack.

1974 Foundation of Gush Emunim (Bloc of the Faithful), religious settlers movement. Golda Meir, Middle East's first woman leader, resigns over post-Yom Kippur War anger.

1975 Amendment to the Trade Act of the USA ties trade benefits to the Soviet Union to freedom of emigration for Jews. United Nations adopts resolution equating Zionism with racism. Rescinded in 1991. Israel becomes an associate member of the European Common Market.

1977 Likud party takes power after Israeli elections, ousting Labour for the first time since independence.

1978 18 September: Israel and Egypt sign comprehensive peace accords at Camp David. Leftist Israelis found Peace Now.

1979 Israel–Egypt Peace Treaty signed. Prime Minister Menachem Begin and President Anwar Sadat are awarded Nobel Peace Prize.

### 1980–2000

1982 Israel's withdrawal from Sinai completed. Operation Peace for Galilee removes PLO fighters from southern Lebanon.

1982 June–December: The Lebanon War.

1983 American Reform Jews formally accept patrilineal descent. Menachem Begin resigns as prime minister, replaced by Yitzhak Shamir.

1984–5 Operations Moses and Joshua: Rescue of Ethiopian Jewry by Israel. Inconclusive elections result in Labour–Likud coalition; rotating prime-ministerial formula.

1987 Beginning of the First Intifada against Israel.

1989 Fall of the Berlin Wall. Four-point peace initiative proposed by Israel.

1990 The Soviet Union relaxes its emigration laws. Thousands leave for Israel.

1990–1 Iraq invades Kuwait, triggering a war between Iraq and Allied United Nations forces.

1991 Operation Solomon rescues most remaining Ethiopian Jews. The Madrid Peace Conference opens in Spain. First bilateral talks between Israeli and Jordanian, Syrian and Palestinian delegations since 1949.

1992 New government headed by Yitzhak Rabin of the Labour party.

1993 13 September: Israel and the PLO sign the Oslo Accords.

1994 26 October: Israel and Jordan sign an official peace treaty.

1994 10 December: Arafat, Rabin and Peres share the Nobel Peace Prize. Palestinian self-government in Gaza Strip and Jericho area.

1995 Broadened Palestinian self-government is implemented in West Bank and Gaza Strip.

1995 4 November: Israeli Prime Minister Yitzhak Rabin is assassinated.

1996 Palestinian Council elected.

1999 Ehud Barak elected Prime Minister of Israel.

### 2000–

2000 24 May: Israel withdraws its forces from southern Lebanon.

2000 Camp David II peace talks between Israel, PLO and USA fail.

2000 29 September: Start of second Palestinian uprising, al-Aqsa Intifada.

2001 Election of Ariel Sharon as Israel's Prime Minister.

2002 Spate of suicide attacks on Israeli towns. Israeli military reoccupation of Palestinian urban centres.

2003 US President George W Bush proposes Israeli–Palestinian roadmap to peace. Arab League re-airs Abdullah Plan for peace.

2005 31 March: Israeli government recognizes the Bnei Menashe people of north-east India as one of the Ten Lost Tribes of Israel.

2005 August: The Government of Israel withdraws military and Jewish settlers from the Gaza Strip.

2006 Prime Minister Ehud Olmert of Israel forms government. Islamist Hamas wins Palestinian elections.

2008 Israel celebrates 60 years of independence.

2009 Barack Obama becomes first US President to host Passover seder in the White House, Washington DC.

2013 Following attacks on Israel from Gaza, debate in the Jewish community about the feasibility of a two-state solution to the Middle East crisis.

*Below* Celebrating Israel Independence Day at the Western Wall, Jerusalem.

# JEWS IN THE ANCIENT WORLD

JEWISH CIVILIZATION BEGAN IN A POLYTHEISITIC CONTEXT IN THE ANCIENT NEAR EAST. ACCORDING TO SCRIPTURE, GOD CALLED ABRAHAM TO GO FROM BABYLONIA TO THE LAND OF CANAAN.

*Above Moses receiving the Ten Commandments, during the 40-year sojourn in the desert. From the 14th-century Spanish Sarajevo Haggadah.*

The history of the Jewish people began in Mesopotamia where successive empires of the ancient world flourished and decayed before the Jews emerged as a separate people. The culture of these civilizations had a profound impact on the Jewish religion – ancient Near Eastern myths were refashioned to serve the needs of the Hebrew people. It appears that the Jews emerged in this milieu as a separate nation between the 19th and 16th centuries BCE. According to the Bible, Abraham was the father of the Jewish people. Initially known as Abram, he came from Ur of the Chaldeans. Together with his family he went to Harran and subsequently to Canaan, later settling in the plain near Hebron. Abraham was followed by Isaac and Jacob, whose son Joseph was sold

*Below The Exodus from Egypt through the Red Sea, a 17th-century painting by Frans Francken the Younger.*

into slavery in Egypt. There he prospered, becoming a vizier in the house of Pharaoh. Eventually the entire Hebrew clan moved to Egypt, where they remained and flourished for centuries before a new Pharaoh decreed that all male Hebrew babies should be put to death.

## THE EXODUS

To persuade Pharaoh to let the Jewish people go, God sent a series of plagues upon the Egyptians. After this devastation, Moses, the leader of the Jewish people, led his kinsfolk out of Egypt. After wandering in the desert for 40 years, the Hebrews finally entered into the land that God had promised them. Under Joshua's leadership, the Hebrews conquered the existing inhabitants, the Canaanites. After Joshua's death the people began to form separate groups. At first there were 12 tribes named after the sons of Jacob. During this period the Hebrews

were ruled by 12 national heroes who served successively as judges.

Frequently the covenant between God and his chosen people was proclaimed at gatherings in national shrines such as Shechem. Such an emphasis on covenantal obligation reinforced the belief that the Jews were the recipients of God's loving kindness. Now in a more settled existence, the covenant expanded to include additional legislation, including the provisions needed for an agricultural community. During this period it became increasingly clear to the Jewish nation that the God of the covenant directed human history – the Exodus and the entry into the Promised Land – were viewed as the unfolding of a divine plan.

## THE PERIOD OF THE JUDGES

Under the judges, God was conceived as the supreme monarch. When some tribes suggested to Gideon that he deserved a formal position of power, he declared that it was impossible for the nation to be ruled by both God and a human

king. None the less, Saul was subsequently elected as king despite the prophet Samuel's warnings against the dangers of usurping God's rule. Later, the Israelite nation divided into two kingdoms. The northern and southern tribes were united only by their allegiance to King David but when his successor, King Solomon, and his son Rehoboam violated many of the ancient traditions, the northern tribes revolted. The reason they gave for this rebellion was the injustice of the monarchy, but in fact they sought to recapture the simple ways of the generation that had escaped from Egypt. It is against this background that the pre-exilic prophets, including Elijah, Elisha, Amos, Hosea, Micah and Isaiah, endeavoured to bring the nation back to the true worship of God.

## DECLINE AND DESTRUCTION
During the 1st millennium BCE the Jews watched their country emerge as a powerful state only to see it sink into spiritual and moral decay. As a punishment for the nation's iniquity,

*Below Babylonian cuneiform tablet from 700–500BCE, with inscription and map of Mesopotamia. In the centre Babylon is surrounded by Assyria and Elam.*

*Above In 70CE, the Romans under Emperor Titus destroyed the Temple in Jerusalem. 15th-century Flemish picture.*

the northern kingdom was devastated by the Assyrians in 722BCE. Two centuries later the southern kingdom fell to the Babylonians. Following the Babylonian conquest in 586BCE the Temple lay in ruins and the people despaired of their fate. Yet, despite defeat and exile, the nation rose from the ashes of the old kingdoms. In the centuries that followed, the Jewish people continued their religious traditions and communal life. Though they had lost their independence, their devotion to God and his law sustained them through suffering and hardship.

## RETURN TO JUDAH
In Babylonia the exiles flourished, keeping their religion alive in the synagogues. These institutions were founded so that Jews could meet together for worship and study; no sacrifices were offered since that was the prerogative of the Jerusalem Temple. In 538BCE King Cyrus of Persia permitted the Jews to return to their former home and the nation was transformed. The Temple was rebuilt and religious reforms were enacted. The period following the death of King Herod in 4BCE was a time of intense anti-Roman feeling among the Jewish population in Judea as well as in the Diaspora. Eventually such hostility led to war, only to be followed by defeat and the destruction of the Second

Temple. In 70CE thousands of Jews were deported. Such devastation, however, did not quell the Jewish hope of ridding the Holy Land of its Roman oppressors. In the 2nd century CE, a messianic rebellion led by Simon Bar Kochba was crushed by Roman forces. Yet despite this defeat, the Pharisees carried on the Jewish tradition through teaching and study at Jabneh, near Jerusalem.

*Below Abraham, father of the Jewish people, preparing to sacrifice his son Isaac, from a 1700s Arabian manuscript.*

# RABBINIC AND MEDIEVAL JUDAISM

THE EMERGENCE OF RABBINIC JUDAISM HAS FUNDAMENTALLY CHANGED THE NATURE OF JUDAISM. FROM THE HELLENISTIC PERIOD TO TODAY THE RABBIS HAVE DOMINATED ALL ASPECTS OF JEWISH LIFE.

From the 1st century BCE Palestinian rabbinic scholars engaged in the interpretation of Scripture. The most important scholar of the early rabbinic period was Yehuda Ha-Nasi (135–*c*.220CE), the head of the Sanhedrin (a group of distinguished Pharisaic scholars), whose main achievement was the redaction of the Mishnah, or 'compendium of Jewish law', in the 2nd century CE. This volume consisted of the discussions and rulings of sages whose teachings had been transmitted orally.

According to the rabbis, the law recorded in the Mishnah was given orally to Moses along with the written law. This implies that there was an infallible chain of transmission from Moses to the leaders of the nation and eventually to the Pharisees.

The Sanhedrin, which had been so fundamental in the compilation of the Mishnah, met in several cities in Galilee, but later settled in the Roman district of Tiberias. Other scholars simultaneously established their own schools in other parts of the country where they applied the Mishnah to everyday life, together with old rabbinic teachings, which had not been incorporated in the Mishnah.

During the 3rd century CE the Roman Empire encountered numerous difficulties including inflation, population decline and a lack of technological development to support the army. In addition, rival generals struggled against one another for power, and the government became increasingly inefficient. Throughout this time of upheaval,

*Above Head of a colossal statue of Constantine the Great, who extended official religious toleration to Christians.*

the Jewish community underwent a similar decline as a result of famine, epidemics and plunder.

### THE RISE OF CHRISTIANITY

At the end of the 3rd century CE, the emperor Diocletian (ruled 284–305CE) inaugurated reforms that strengthened the Roman empire. In addition, Diocletian introduced measures to repress the spread of Christianity, which had become a serious challenge to the official religion of the empire. However Diocletian's successor, Constantine the Great (ruled 306–37CE), reversed his predecessor's hostile stance and also extended official toleration to Christians in the empire.

By this stage Christianity had succeeded in gaining a substantial number of adherents among the urban population; eventually Constantine became more involved in Church affairs and just before his death he himself was baptized. The Christianization of the empire continued throughout the century and by the early 400s CE Christianity was fully established as the state religion.

*Below Medieval migration of Jews showing their expulsion from Spain and some Slavic countries and movement to Islamic and other lands.*

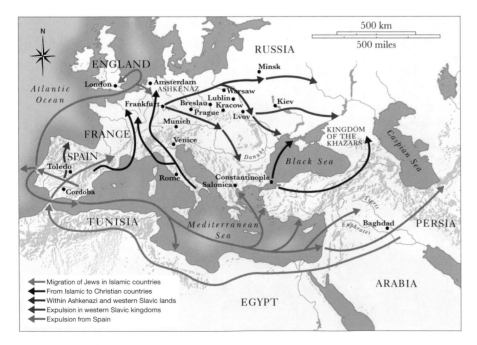

## IN THE DIASPORA

By the 6th century CE the Jews had become largely a Diaspora people. Despite the loss of a homeland, they were unified by a common heritage: law, liturgy and shared traditions bound together the scattered communities stretching from Spain to Persia and from Poland to Africa. Living among Christians and Muslims, the Jewish community was reduced to a minority group and its marginal status resulted in repeated persecution. Though there were times of tolerance and creative activity, the threats of exile and death were always present in Jewish consciousness during this period.

## UNDER ISLAM

Within the Islamic world, Jews along with Christians were recognized as 'Peoples of the Book' and were guaranteed religious toleration, judicial autonomy and exemption from the military. In turn they were required to accept the supremacy of the Islamic state. During the first two centuries of Islamic rule under the Umayyad and Abbasid caliphates, Muslim leaders confirmed the authority of traditional Babylonian institutions. When the Arabs con-

*Left A 13th-century South German illumination showing Moses receiving the Ten Commandments, from the Regensburg Pentateuch.*

*Right A Jewish scholar presents a translation of an Arabic treatise to Philippe d'Anjou, 13th century.*

quered Babylonia, they officially recognized the position of the Jewish exilarch, who for centuries had been the ruler of Babylonian Jewry. By the Abbasid period, the exilarch shared his power with the heads of the rabbinical academies which had for centuries been the major centres of rabbinic learning.

During the 8th century CE messianic movements appeared in the Persian Jewish community, which led to armed uprisings against Muslim authority. Such revolts were quickly crushed, but an even more serious threat to traditional Jewish life was posed later in the century by the emergence of an anti-rabbinic sect, the Karaites. This group was founded in Babylonia in the 760s CE by Anan ben David. The growth of Karaism provoked the rabbis to attack it as a heretical movement since these various groups rejected rabbinic law and formulated their own legislation.

## THE DECENTRALIZATION OF RABBINIC JUDAISM

By the 8th century CE the Muslim empire began to undergo a process of disintegration; this process was accompanied by a decentralization of rabbinic Judaism. The academies of Babylonia began to lose their hold on the Jewish scholarly world, and in many places rabbinic schools were established in which rabbinic sources were studied. In the Holy Land, Tiberias was the location of an important rabbinical academy as well as the centre of the masoretic scholars who produced the standard text of the Bible. But it was in Spain that the Jewish community was to

attain the greatest level of achievement in literature, philosophy, theology and mysticism.

In their campaigns the Muslims did not manage to conquer all of Europe – many countries remained under Christian rule, as did much of the Byzantine empire. In Christian Europe, Jewish study took place in a number of important towns such as Mainz and Worms in the Rhineland and Troyes and Sens in northern France. In such an environment the study of the Talmud reached great heights; in Germany and northern France scholars known as 'the Tosafists' used new methods of talmudic interpretation. In addition Ashkenazic Jews of this period composed religious poetry modelled on the liturgical compositions of 5th- and 6th-centuries CE Israel.

Yet, despite such an efflorescence of Jewish life, the expulsion of the Jews from the countries in which they lived became a dominant policy of Christian Europe. They were driven out of Rome in 139BCE, from England in 1290, from Germany in 1348, from Spain in 1492 and from many other states. Repeatedly, Jewish communities throughout Europe suffered violent attack, and Jewish massacre became a frequent occurrence.

# JEWS IN THE EARLY MODERN PERIOD

DURING THE EARLY MODERN PERIOD, JEWISH SCHOLARS CONTINUED TO CONTRIBUTE TO JEWISH LIFE. HOWEVER THE LONGING FOR MESSIANIC DELIVERANCE CONTINUED TO ANIMATE JEWISH CONSCIOUSNESS.

By the end of the 14th century political instability in Christian Europe led to the massacre of many Jewish communities in Castile and Aragon. Fearing for their lives, thousands of Jews converted to Christianity at the end of the century. Two decades later Spanish rulers introduced the Castilian laws that segregated Jews from their Christian neighbours. In the following year a public disputation was held in Tortosa about the doctrine of the Messiah; as a result increased pressure was applied to the Jewish population to convert. Those who became Maranos, or apostates, found life much easier, but by the 15th century anti-Jewish sentiment again became a serious problem. In 1480 King Ferdinand and Queen Isabella of Spain established the Inquisition to determine whether former Jews practised Judaism in

*Below Many Jews fled Spain to escape the tortures of the Inquisition, shown here in a 19th-century engraving.*

secret. To escape such persecution many Maranos sought refuge in various parts of the Ottoman empire.

## RABBINIC SAGES

Prominent among the rabbinic scholars of this period was Joseph ben Ephraim Caro (1488–1575), who emigrated from Spain to the Balkans. In the 1520s he commenced a study of Jewish law, *The House of Joseph*, based on previous codes of Jewish law. In addition, he composed a shorter work, the *Shulkhan Arukh*, which has become the authoritative code of law in the Jewish world. While working on the *Shulkhan Arukh*, Caro emigrated to Safed in Israel, which had become a major centre of Jewish religious life. Talmudic academies were established and small groups engaged in the study of Kabbalistic (mystical) literature as they piously awaited the coming of the Messiah. In this centre of Kabbalistic activity one of the greatest mystics of Safed, Moses Cordovero (1522–70),

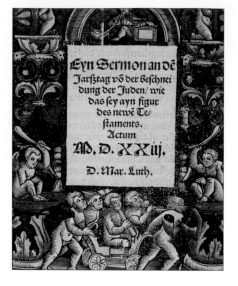

*Above 16th-century Jews often found life insecure, as evidenced by this sermon of Martin Luther condemning the Jews. His anti-Semitism had a persistent influence on German attitudes towards Jews.*

collected, organized and interpreted the teachings of earlier mystical authors. Later in the 16th century, Kabbalistic speculation was transformed by the greatest mystic of Safed, Isaac Luria (1534–72).

## THE MYSTICAL MESSIAH

By the beginning of the 17th century Lurianic mysticism had made an important impact on Sephardic Jewry, and messianic expectations had also become a central feature of Jewish life. In this milieu the arrival of a self-proclaimed messianic king, Shabbetai Tzvi (1626–76), brought about a transformation of Jewish life and thought. After living in various cities, he travelled to Gaza where he encountered Nathan Benjamin Levi, who believed he was the Messiah. His messiahship was proclaimed in 1665, and Nathan sent letters to Jews in the Diaspora asking them to recognize Shabbetai Tzvi as their redeemer.

Eventually Shabbetai was brought to court and given the choice between conversion and death. In the face of this alternative, he converted to Islam. Such an act of

apostasy scandalized most of his followers, but others continued to revere him as the Messiah. In the following century the most important Shabbetean sect was led by Jacob Frank, who believed himself to be the incarnation of Shabbetai.

## PERSECUTION

During this period Poland had become a great centre of scholarship. In Polish academies scholars collected together the legal interpretations of previous authorities and composed commentaries on the *Shulkhan Arukh*. However, in the midst of this general prosperity, the Polish Jewish community was subject to a series of massacres carried out by the Cossacks of the Ukraine, Crimean Tartars and Ukrainian peasants. In 1648 Bogdan Chmielnicki (1595–1657), head of the Cossacks, instigated an insurrection against the Polish gentry, and Jews were slaughtered in these revolts.

Elsewhere in Europe this period witnessed Jewish persecution and oppression. Despite the positive con-

*Below A 17th-century engraving of Shabbetai Tzvi, a charismatic from Turkey and self-proclaimed Messiah.*

### THE ORIGINS OF HASIDISM (ALSO SPELLED HASSIDISM OR CHASIDISM)

By the middle of the 18th century the Jewish community had suffered numerous waves of persecution and

was deeply dispirited by the conversion of Shabbetai Tzvi. In this environment the Hasidic movement sought to revitalize Jewish life. The founder of this new sect was Israel ben Eliezer, known as the Ba'al Shem Tov (1700–60), who was born in southern Poland. Legend relates that he performed various miracles and instructed his disciples in Kabbalistic lore. By the 1740s he had attracted many disciples who passed on his teaching. After his death, Dov Baer became the leader of his sect and Hasidism spread to southern Poland, the Ukraine and Lithuania.

*Left The Ba'al Shem Tov (Israel ben Eliezer), founder of Hasidism.*

tact between Italian humanists and Jews, Christian anti-Semitism frequently led to persecution and suffering. In the 16th century the Counter-Reformation Church attempted to isolate the Jewish community. The Talmud was burned in 1553, and two years later Pope Paul IV reinstated the segregationist edict of the Fourth Lateran Council, forcing Jews to live in ghettos and barring them from most areas of economic life. In Germany the growth of Protestantism frequently led to adverse conditions for the Jewish population. Though Martin Luther was initially well disposed to the Jews, he soon came to realize the Jewish community was intent on remaining true to its faith. As a consequence, he composed a virulent attack on the Jews.

By the mid-17th century, Dutch Jews had attained importance in trade and finance. Maranos and Ashkenazi Jews flourished in Amsterdam. In this milieu Jewish cultural activity grew: Jewish writers published works of drama, theology and mystical lore.

Though Jews in Holland were not granted full rights as citizens, they nevertheless enjoyed religious freedom, personal protection and liberty in economic affairs.

*Below The Haari synagogue in Safed, home of rabbinic scholar Joseph Caro and mystic Isaac Luria.*

# JEWS IN THE MODERN WORLD

JEWISH EMANCIPATION IN THE 18TH CENTURY LED TO A REVOLUTION IN JEWISH LIFE. HOWEVER THE RISE OF ANTI-SEMITICISM IN THE 19TH CENTURY LED TO TERRIBLE CONSEQUENCES IN THE 1930S AND 40S.

During the late 18th century the treatment of Jews in central Europe improved owing to the influence of Christian polemicists.

## JEWISH EMANCIPATION

Within this environment Jewish emancipation gathered force. The Jewish philosopher Moses Mendelssohn (1729–86) advocated the modernization of Jewish life. To further this advance he translated the Pentateuch into German so that Jews would be able to speak the language of the country in which they lived. Following his example, a number of followers known as the *maskilim* fostered the Haskalah, or Jewish Enlightenment, which encouraged Jews to abandon medieval forms of life and thought.

## REFORM JUDAISM

Paralleling this development, reformers encouraged the modernization of the Jewish liturgy and reform of Jewish education. Although such changes were denounced by the

*Below Proclamation of the Independence of the State of Israel by PM David Ben-Gurion, Tel Aviv, 14 May 1948.*

Orthodox establishment, Reform Judaism spread throughout Europe. In 1844 the first Reform synod took place in Brunswick; followed by a conference in 1845 in Frankfurt. At this gathering one of the more conservative rabbis, Zacharias Frankel (1801–75), expressed dissatisfaction with progressive reforms to Jewish worship. He resigned and established a Jewish theological seminary in Breslau. Eventually this approach to the tradition led to the creation of Conservative Judaism. In 1846 a third synod took place at Breslau, but the revolution and its aftermath brought about the cessation of these activities until 1868, when another synod took place at Cassel.

In the United States, Reform Judaism became an important feature of Jewish life. The most prominent of the early reformers was Isaac Mayer Wise (1819–1900), who came to Albany, New York from Bavaria. Later he went to Cincinnati, Ohio where he published a new Reform prayer book as well as several Jewish newspapers. In 1869 the first Central Conference of American Rabbis was held in Philadelphia; followed in 1873 by the founding of the Union of American Hebrew Congregations. In 1875 the Hebrew Union College was established to train rabbinical students for Reform congregations.

## ZIONISM

In eastern Europe conditions were less conducive to emancipation, and a series of pogroms took place in Russia in 1881–2. After these events, many Jews emigrated to the United States as well as Palestine. By the late

*Above Theodor Herzl, founder of political Zionism, on a bridge in Basle during the 5th Zionist Congress.*

1880s the idea of a Jewish homeland had spread throughout Europe. At the first Zionist Congress at Basle in 1897, Theodor Herzl (1860–1904) called for a national home based on international law.

By 1900 a sizeable number of Jews had emigrated to Palestine. After World War I, Jews in Palestine organized a National Assembly and an Executive Council. By 1929 the Jewish community numbered 160,000, and this increased in the next ten years to 500,000. At this time Palestine's population was composed of about one million Arabs consisting of peasants and a number of landowners, plus the Jewish population. In 1929 the Arab community rioted following a dispute about Jewish access to the Western Wall of the ancient Temple. This caused the British to curtail both Jewish immigration and purchase of Arab land.

By the 1920s Labour Zionism had become the dominant force in Palestinian Jewish life; in 1930 various socialist and Labour groups joined together in the Israel Labour Party. Within the Zionist movement a right-wing segment criticized Chaim Weizmann, President of the World Zionist Organization, who was committed to co-operation with the British. Vladimir Jabotinsky, leader

*Above* Scene at St Petersburg railway station in 1891 as many Jews fled from anti-Semitism in Russia.

of the Union of Zionist Revisionists, stressed that the central aim of the Zionist movement was the establishment of an independent state in the whole of Palestine. In 1937 a British Royal Commission proposed that Palestine be partitioned into a Jewish and Arab state with a British zone; this recommendation was accepted by Zionists but rejected by the Arabs.

In 1939, a British Government White Paper rejected the concept of partition, limited Jewish immigration, and decreed Palestine would become independent in ten years.

THE HOLOCAUST
As these events unfolded in the Middle East, Jews in Germany were confronted by increasing hostility. The Nazis gained control of the government and curtailed civil liberties. In November 1938 they organized an onslaught against the Jewish population known as *Kristallnacht*, a prelude to the Holocaust. Hitler invaded Poland in September 1939, and later that year incorporated much of the country into Germany; more than 600,000 Jews were gathered into a large area in Poland. This was

*Right* An Arab anti-Zionist demonstration in Palestine under the British mandate, 8 March 1920.

followed by the invasion of Russia in 1941, and the Nazis used mobile killing battalions, the *Einsatzgruppen*, to destroy Russian Jewry. In time fixed killing centres were created at six death camps where millions of Jews and others were murdered.

During the war and afterwards, the British prevented illegal immigrants entering the Holy Land, and Jews in Palestine campaigned against this policy. By 19 November 1947 the General Assembly of the United Nations endorsed a plan of partition, and the Arabs then attacked Jewish settlements. In May 1948, David Ben-Gurion (1886–1973) read out the Scroll of Independence of the Jewish state. Immediately a government was formed, and the Arabs stepped up their assault. Following the War of Independence, armistice talks were held and agreements signed with Egypt, Lebanon, Transjordan and Syria. Later President Gamal Abdel Nasser refused Israeli ships access to the Gulf of Aqaba in 1956, seized the Suez Canal and formed a pact with Saudi Arabia and various Arab states. In response, Israel launched a strike, conquering Sinai and opening the sea route to Aqaba. These events were followed by the Six Day War in 1967, the Yom

*Above* Existential philosopher Martin Buber deeply influenced Jewish religious thought with his I and Thou *(1923)*.

Kippur War in 1973, and in 1982 an Israeli offensive against the PLO in Southern Lebanon.

In the ensuing years, hostility between Jews and Arabs has intensified. The *intifada* coupled with repeated suicide bombing led to the creation of a massive wall of defence in the Occupied Territories. Rocket attacks on Israel from Gaza in 2012 has hardened Israeli opinion and made a two-state solution more difficult. For Jews worldwide, the defence of Israel in the face of Arab opposition has become a major feature of contemporary Jewish life.

# CHAPTER 1
# ANCIENT JUDAISM

According to Scripture, Abraham was chosen by God to create a new nation. His descendants were to be as numerous as the stars in heaven. The Book of Genesis describes the faith of the patriarchs – Abraham, Isaac and Jacob – and the subsequent history of the ancient Hebrews.

Faith in one God sustained them in Canaan and their long sojourn in Egypt. They were enslaved by the Egyptian Pharaoh, but rescued by Moses who led them into the desert for 40 years. Under Joshua's leadership, the Jewish people conquered the Canaanites and established a monarchy. With the creation of a Temple in Jerusalem, a new form of Judaism emerged, rooted in cultic observance. The emergence of the prophets brought about a profound change in religious orientation with stress on moral action. Under the influence of Hellenism, the Jewish faith underwent further change. In the Northern Kingdom the Samaritans developed their own interpretation of the faith. As time passed, the Jewish nation divided into three major groups – the Sadducees, Pharisees and Essenes – with different religious orientations.

*Opposite Moses and the Burning Bush. A 2nd-century painting from Dura-Europos, Syria, a synagogue with extraordinarily fine frescoes that was uncovered virtually intact in 1932.*

*Above A 19th-century print of the ancient city of Jerusalem showing the city walls and the magnificent Temple of King Solomon towering above it all.*

# ANCIENT HEBREWS

THE RELIGION OF THE ANCIENT HEBREWS WAS BASED ON TRADITIONS
SURROUNDING THE PATRIARCHS, THE EXILE IN EGYPT AND GOD'S
REDEMPTION OF HIS CHOSEN PEOPLE FROM BONDAGE.

The birth of the Jewish people occurred in ancient Mesopotamia. According to Scripture, God called Abraham to travel from Ur of the Chaldeans to Canaan where he promised to make his descendants as numerous as the stars in heaven.

### THE ANCIENT NEAR EAST

The rise of ancient Mesopotamian civilization occurred at the end of the 4th millennium BCE in southern Mesopotamia, where the Sumerians created city states, each with its local god. During the 3rd millennium BCE waves of Semitic peoples settled amid the Sumerians. These Semites, known as Akkadians, identified some of their gods with the Sumerian deities. For these peoples, life was under these gods' control. To obtain happiness, it was essential to keep the gods in good humour through worship and sacrifice.

*Below Jacob dreamt of a ladder to heaven during his flight from his brother Esau. 16th-century painting by Nicolas Dipre.*

*Right Abraham receives the divine promise that his descendants would be as numerous as the stars. A 2nd-century wall painting from Dura-Europos, Syria.*

### THE PATRIARCHS

It was in this polytheistic milieu that the Jews emerged as a separate people in the 19th–16th centuries BCE. According to the biblical narrative in Genesis, Abraham was the father of the Jewish nation. Originally known as Abram, he came from Ur of the Chaldeans – a Sumerian city of Mesopotamia. Together with his father Terah, his wife Sarai, and his nephew Lot, he travelled to Harran, a trading centre in northern Syria. There his father died, and God called upon him to go to Canaan: 'Go from your country and your kindred and your father's house to the land I will show you. And I will make of you a great nation.' (Genesis 12:1–2).

Abraham's belief in one God constituted a radical break from the past. Unlike the Sumerians and Akkadians, who believed in a pantheon of gods, Abraham was committed to the God who had revealed himself to him and ruled over heaven and earth. Scripture records that God made a covenant with Abraham symbolized by an act of circumcision: 'You shall be circumcised in the flesh of your foreskins and it shall be a sign of the covenant between me and you.' (Genesis 17:11). Later, God tested Abraham's dedication by ordering him to sacrifice Isaac, only telling him at the last moment to refrain. Repeatedly in the Book of Genesis God appeared to Abraham, reassuring him of his destiny. Similarly, God revealed himself to Abraham's son, Isaac, and to his grandson, Jacob.

Like Abraham, Jacob was told that his offspring would inherit the land of Canaan and fill the earth. When Jacob travelled to Harran, he had a vision of a ladder rising to heaven: 'And behold, the angels of God were ascending and descending on it! And behold, the

*Below The Plagues of Egypt. An illumination from a Bohemian Haggadah of 1728.*

## THE JOSEPH NARRATIVES

The history of the three patriarchs is followed by a cycle of stories about Jacob's son Joseph. Like his ancestors, Joseph believed in a providential God who guided his destiny. When Joseph was in Shechem helping his brothers

tend his family's flocks he angered them by recounting dreams in which they bowed down before him. They reacted by plotting his death. Joseph was eventually taken to Egypt, where he became Pharaoh's chief minister. When his brothers came before him to buy grain because of a famine in Canaan, he revealed his true identity and God's providential care.

The Jewish people were later enslaved in Egypt, an event leading to the Exodus.

*Left This remarkable 19th-century Russian painting has Jacob's eldest son Reuben showing him Joseph's coat.*

Lord stood above it and said, "I am the Lord, the God of Abraham your father and the god of Isaac; the land on which you lie I will give to you and to your descendants, and your descendants shall be like the dust of the earth."' (Genesis 28:12–18).

### THE EXODUS

The biblical narrative continues with an account of the deliverance of God's chosen people from Egyptian bondage. Here again, Scripture emphasizes that God is active in human history. The Book of Exodus relates that God revealed himself to Moses and commanded that he deliver the ancient Hebrews from bondage: 'I am the God of your father, the God of Abraham, the God of Isaac, and the God of Jacob ... I have seen the affliction of my people who are in Egypt, and have heard their cry because of their taskmasters. I know their sufferings ... Come, I will send you to Pharaoh that you may bring forth my people, the sons of Israel, out of Egypt.' (Exodus 3:6–7, 10)

In order to persuade Pharaoh that he should let the Jewish people go, God sent plagues on the Egyptians,

culminating in the slaying of every Egyptian first-born son. After the final plague, Pharaoh released the Israelites, and they fled without even waiting for their bread to rise. However, their perils did not end: Pharaoh changed his mind and sent his forces in pursuit. When the Israelites came to an expanse of water, it seemed that they were trapped. Yet miraculously it was converted to dry land so that they were able to escape. For the ancient Israelites, the belief in a providential

God who rescues his people from disaster became a central feature of the faith and is celebrated each year at the Passover festival.

### REVELATION ON SINAI

This band of free people then entered the wilderness of Sinai, where God performed miracles to provide them with food and water. After travelling for about 90 days, they encamped before Mount Sinai. God called Moses up to the top of the mountain and told him that if his people would listen to him and keep his covenant they would become God's special people. Moses remained on the mountain for 40 days; at the end of this period, he returned with two tablets of stone on which were inscribed God's laws. These commandments served as the basis for Jewish life as they wandered through the desert for 40 years. Convinced that they were God's chosen people, the ancient Hebrews worshipped the Lord of creation who had chosen them from among all peoples and given them his sacred law so that they could become a priestly nation.

*Below When the people of Israel danced before the Golden Calf, Moses condemned them for setting up an idol. 16th-century fresco by Raphael.*

# TEMPLE JUDAISM

THE LIFE OF THE JEWISH NATION WAS ANIMATED BY WORSHIP AND PRAYER. ONCE THEY HAD SETTLED IN THE PROMISED LAND, JEWS OFFERED SACRIFICES IN THE TEMPLE IN JERUSALEM.

During the early history of the nation, the patriarchs prayed to God and offered sacrifices on high places. Later the Jewish people worshipped God in a portable sanctuary. There sacrifices were offered to the Lord of the universe who had delivered his people from slavery. Yet, in time this simple form of worship was replaced by an elaborate cultic system in the Jerusalem Temple. This magnificent structure and its surrounding buildings were constructed by King Solomon in the 10th century BCE.

## THE SANCTUARY

For the ancient Hebrews, God was both transcendent and imminent. He had created the universe, yet was intimately involved in the life of his people. Throughout the Genesis narrative, the patriarchs turned to him in prayer. Worship took many forms: petition, confession, praise, thanksgiving, adoration and intercession. In addition, the patriarchs offered sacrifice to God on high places.

Later, Scripture records that Moses made a portable shrine (sanctuary), following God's instructions (Exodus 25–27). This structure travelled with the Israelites in the desert, and it was placed in the centre of the camp in an open courtyard 1,000 cubits (a cubit is the approximate length of a forearm) by 50 cubits (about 1500 X 75 ft/457 X 23m) in size. The fence surrounding it consisted of wooden pillars from which a cloth curtain was suspended. Located in the eastern half of the courtyard, the sanctuary measured 50 cubits by 10 cubits (about 75 X 15 ft/23 X 4.5m). At its end stood the Holy of Holies, which was separated by a veil hanging on five

*Above Two rabbis celebrating Pesach (Passover), from the* Agada Pascatis, *a 15th-century Haggadah manuscript.*

wooden pillars on which were woven images of the cherubim. Inside the Holy of Holies was the Ark of the Covenant, the table on which the shewbread, or 12 loaves representing the 12 tribes of Israel, was placed, the incense altar, and the menorah, or 'candelabrum'. In the courtyard there was also an outer altar on which sacrifices were offered, as well as a brass laver for priests.

## THE JERUSALEM TEMPLE

Eventually this structure was superseded by the Temple, which was built by King Solomon on Mount

*Below King Solomon overseeing the construction of the Temple in Jerusalem. From an illuminated 16th-century French Bible.*

### A NATIONAL CENTRE

Through the centuries the Temple was viewed as a national centre; moreover, since it was the abode of the Ark, it was considered to be the site of the revelation of the Divine Presence and the preferred place for prayer. For this reason individual worshippers directed their supplications towards the Temple even from afar. There the people also gathered in times of distress when the priests would weep between the vestibule and the altar. For the prophets, the Temple Mount (Mount Zion) was the mountain of the Lord, and the Temple was the house of the God of Jacob and the Lord's house. It was the place where God's name was called. In the words of the prophet Jeremiah, it was 'a glorious throne set on high from the beginning.' (Jeremiah 17:12).

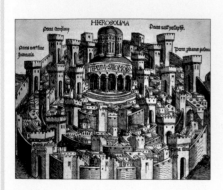

*Left A woodcut of Jerusalem and the Temple of Solomon by Melchior Wolgemuth, from the* Nuremberg Chronicle, *1493.*

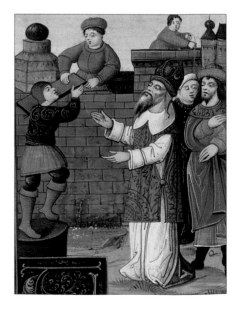

*Right Preparations for the Passover, which in ancient times was observed in the Temple in Jerusalem. Bible illustration, 1470, by Leonardo Bellini.*

Moriah in Jerusalem in the 10th century BCE. Acting as the focus of prayer in ancient Israel, the Temple reoriented religious life and took the place of simpler forms of worship. The two principal sources for the plan of the Temple are 1 Kings 6–8 and 2 Chronicles 2–4. Standing within a royal compound, which also consisted of a palace, a Hall of Judgement, the Hall of Cedars, and a house for Solomon's wife, the Temple was 60 cubits long, 20 cubits wide, and 30 cubits high (about 88 x 30 x 46 ft/27 x 9 x 14m).

The main Temple was surrounded by a three-storeyed building divided into chambers with storeys connected by trap doors – these were probably storerooms for the Temple treasures. The main building consisted of an inner room – the Holy of Holies – on the west, and an outer room measuring 20 by 40 cubits (about 30 x 60 ft/9 x 18m) on the east. Around the Temple was a walled-in compound. At the entrance to the Temple stood two massive bronze pillars. Within the Holy of Holies stood the Ark, which contained the Two Tablets of the Covenant with the Ten Commandments.

In the outer room stood an incense altar, the table for the shewbread, and ten lampstands made of gold. In front of the Temple stood a bronze basin supported by 12 bronze cattle. A bronze altar also stood in the courtyard, which was used for various sacrifices.

## THE LEVITES

In addition to sacrificial worship, it was customary for the Levites who served in the Temple to sing to the accompaniment of lyres with harps and cymbals. Many psalms in the Bible are ascribed to these Levite singers.

Primarily, the Temple was a place of assembly for the entire people for purposes of sacrifice, prayer and thanksgiving. They would come to Jerusalem to bring sin and guilt offerings as well as burnt offerings, peace offerings and meal offerings either in fulfilment of vows or as offerings of thanksgiving. These sacrifices had to be eaten within a day or two of their slaughter, and were apparently brought to the accompaniment of songs and in procession.

## FESTIVAL WORSHIP

Special importance was attached to public processions in celebration of festivals. The people travelled to the Temple to worship before the Lord on Sabbaths and New Moons, at appointed seasons, and during the three pilgrim festivals (Pesach, Sukkot and Shavuot). Coming from Judah and beyond, the festal crowd would proceed in a throng with shouts and songs of thanksgiving; the procession was accompanied by the playing of musical instruments. The

right to serve in the Temple was assigned to the priests who were descended from Aaron, who were assisted by the Levites. The king enjoyed a status of holiness in the Temple, but in contrast to the priests, he was not permitted either to enter the sanctuary or to burn incense.

*Below Coin depicting the kind of lyre that may have been used in the Temple in Jerusalem, dated 134–5CE, the third year of Bar Kochba's war against the Romans.*

# PROPHETIC JUDAISM

THE PROPHETS OF ANCIENT ISRAEL WERE THE VOICE OF CONSCIENCE.
REPEATEDLY THEY WARNED THE PEOPLE TO TURN FROM THEIR EVIL WAYS
AND EMBRACE THE COVENANT IN ACCORDANCE WITH GOD'S WILL.

Once the ancient Hebrews settled in the Promised Land, they were ruled over by a series of judges. Eventually, a monarchy was established, at first over the entire country; and later, when there were two kingdoms (Israel in the north and Judah in the south), two royal houses reigned over their respective kingdoms. As time passed, a series of prophets emerged who pronounced against the evils of the nation. Prophetic Judaism championed the rule of justice and God's determination to punish his people for their iniquity unless they turned from their evil ways.

### THE NORTHERN KINGDOM
In the 8th century BCE, Israel prospered for 40 years. Towards the end of Jeroboam II's reign, Amos, a shepherd from Tekoa who firmly differentiated himself from the official cultic prophets, proclaimed that

*Above* View of the River Tel and Tekoa, a village in the hills south of Jerusalem. The prophet Amos was born in Tekoa.

Israelite society had become morally corrupt. Many Israelites had become rich, but at the expense of the poor. Israel had sinned, he declared:

because they sell the righteous
   for silver
and the needy for a pair of shoes –
they that trample the head
   of the poor
into the dust of the earth,
and turn aside the way
   of the afflicted.
   (Amos 2: 6–7)

Amos's later contemporary, the prophet Hosea, echoed these dire predictions. Israel had gone astray and would be punished. Yet through personal tragedy – the infidelity of his wife, Gomer – Hosea was able to offer words of consolation and hope. Just as Hosea's love for his wife had been rejected, so God's love for Israel had been despised. But despite the coming devastation, God would not cease to love his chosen people.

Just as Hosea could not give up his wife, God could not abandon Israel: 'How can I hand you over, O Israel! My heart recoils within me, my compassion grows warm and tender.' (Hosea 11:8)

### THE DESTRUCTION OF ISRAEL
As predicted by these pre-exilic Northern prophets, Amos and Hosea, the nation's fate was sealed. God had threatened destruction unless the people repented.

*Left* A stone stele showing two Assyrians driving a chariot, 8th century BCE.

At the beginning of the 8th century BCE the Assyrian King Shalmaneser V (727–722BCE) conquered Israel's capital Samaria after a siege of two years. The annals of Shalmaneser's successor, Sargon II (ruled 721–705BCE), record that 27,290 Israelites were deported as a result of this conquest. This marked the end of the northern kingdom. Following this assault, the kingdom of Judah was under threat.

*Below* According to Scripture, the tribes were descended from Jacob's sons, apart from Ephraim and Manasseh, who were sons of Jacob's son Joseph. Benjamin and Judah were in what became the southern kingdom of Judah, and the others in the northern kingdom of Samaria.

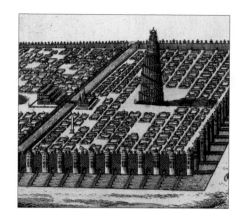

*Above An 18th-century engraving of the Tower of Babel, the Hanging Gardens and the Royal Palace, Babylon.*

## THE SOUTHERN KINGDOM

To avoid a similar fate in the south, King Ahaz of Judah (c.735–720BCE) continued to pay tribute to Assyria and encouraged the nation to worship Assyrian gods. However, the prophet Isaiah was deeply concerned about such idolatrous practices. He believed the collapse of Israel was God's punishment for sinfulness, and he foresaw a similar fate for Judah. Isaiah warned his country that God was not satisfied with empty ritual in the Temple:

What to me is the multitude of
    your sacrifices? says the Lord.
I have had enough of burnt offerings
    of rams and the fat of fed beasts;
I do not delight in the blood of bulls,
    or of lambs, or of he-goats.
    (Isaiah 1:11)

A contemporary of Isaiah, the prophet Micah, also criticized the people for their iniquity and foretold destruction:

Hear this, you heads of the house
    of Jacob
and rulers of the house of Israel,
who abhor justice and pervert
    all equity ...
because of you Zion shall be
    ploughed as a field;
Jerusalem shall become a heap of
    ruins. (Micah 3:9,12)

Ahaz, however, refused to listen to these words; trusting in his own political alliances, he believed his kingdom was secure.

In the next century, the prophet Jeremiah similarly warned that the southern kingdom would eventually be devastated by foreign powers. The Lord, he declared, had this message for the southern kingdom:

Break up your fallow ground
and sow not among thorns.
Circumcise yourselves to the Lord,
remove the foreskins of your hearts,

O men of Judah and inhabitants
    of Jerusalem;
lest my wrath go forth like fire
and burn with none to quench it,
because of the evil of your doings.

Declare in Judah, and proclaim
    in Jerusalem, and say,
'Blow the trumpet through
    the land';
cry aloud and say,
'Assemble and let us go into the
    fortified cities!'
Raise a standard toward Zion,
flee for safety, stay not,
for I bring evil from the north,
and great destruction.
    (Jeremiah 4:3–6)

## DESTRUCTION AND EXILE

In the following century Isaiah, Micah and Jeremiah's predictions were fulfilled: after a siege of 18 months, Jerusalem was conquered in 586BCE; all the main buildings were destroyed, King Zedekiah of Judah (597–86BCE) was blinded and exiled to Babylon.

The anguish of the people facing the tragedy of Babylonian conquest and captivity is reflected in the Book of Lamentations. Here the exiles

*Right Hosea was a compassionate prophet who exhorted the people of Israel to reform. A panel from Sienna Cathedral, 1308.*

bemoaned their fate as predicted by the prophets. The nation had betrayed the covenant and God poured out his wrath as he warned. Reflecting on their holy city, Jerusalem, they declared:

How lonely sits the city that was
    full of people!
How like a widow she has become,
She that was great among
    the nations! ...
The roads to Zion mourn,
for none come
    to the appointed feasts;
all her gates are desolate,
her priests groan;
her maidens have been
    dragged away
and she herself suffers bitterly.
    (Lamentations 1:1,4)

# HELLENISTIC JUDAISM

GREEK CIVILIZATION HAD A PROFOUND IMPACT ON JEWRY, AFFECT-
ING ALL ASPECTS OF JEWISH LIFE. YET THESE CHANGES EVOKED A FIERCE
RESPONSE FROM PIOUS JEWS LOYAL TO THE TRADITION.

Although it is possible that there was some contact between Greeks and the ancient Hebrews, it was not until the 4th century BCE, during the reign of Alexander the Great (336–323BCE), that Greek civilization had a significant impact on Jewish life. The Hellenistic period was thus marked by the increasing influence of Greek ideas on the Jewish tradition.

## THE HELLENISTIC PERIOD

During the centuries after Alexander the Great's reign, Palestine was part of Hellenistic kingdoms, first of Ptolemaic Egypt and then of Seleucid Syria. In the first third of the 2nd century BCE a group of Hellenizing Jews seized power in Jerusalem. Led by wealthy Jewish aristocrats who were attracted to Hellenism, their influence was primarily social rather than cultural and religious. Later, Jason the high priest (175–172BCE) established Jerusalem as a Greek city, Antioch-at-Jerusalem, with Greek educational institutions, such as the gymnasium.

*Below A 2nd-century CE coin of Antiochus IV Epiphanes, the Seleucid king who caused the Maccabean revolt.*

However, Jason was only a moderate Hellenizer compared with his successor as high priest, Menelaus, whose succession provoked a civil war. The Tobiads supported Menelaus, whereas the masses favoured Jason. It was these Hellenizers, including Menelaus and his followers, who influenced the Seleucid King Antiochus IV Epiphanes (175–164BCE) to undertake his persecutions of Jews in order to crush the rebellion of the Hasideans.

## GREEK INFLUENCE

Yet, despite such rebellion the influence of Hellenism was widespread in both Palestine and the Diaspora. Greek was substituted for Hebrew and Aramaic; Greek personal names were frequently adopted; Greek educational institutions were created; there was an efflorescence of Jewish Hellenistic literature and philosophy; and syncretism was widespread. The most obvious instance of Greek influence took place in the creation of Jewish literature during the Hellenistic period. The Jewish wisdom writer Ben Sira, for example, includes a number of aphorisms borrowed from Greek sources. The Testament of Joseph and the Book of Judith show Greek influence. Similarly, the Book of Tobit shows Hellenistic influence in the form of its romance. In his paraphrase of the Bible, the Jewish historian made numerous changes. Abraham, for example, is presented as worthy of Greek political and philosophical ideals; Samson is an Aristotelian-like, great-souled man; Saul is a kind of Achilles; and Solomon is like Oedipus.

*Above The battle of the Maccabees during the Hasmonean revolt by Jean Fouquet for Jewish historian Josephus's Antiquities of the Jews.*

## HELLENISM IN THE DIASPORA

It seems that there was no systematic pattern of Hellenizing in the Diaspora. Indeed, some Alexandrian Jewish writers argued that the Greeks had borrowed from the Jews. The Jewish Peripatetic philosopher Aristobulus asserted in the 2nd century BCE that Homer, Hesiod, Pythagoras, Socrates and Plato were all acquainted with a translation of the Torah into Greek. The first significant Graeco-Jewish historian, Eupolemus, reported that Moses taught the alphabet to the Jews, who then passed it on to the Phoenicians who transmitted it to the Greeks. The 1st-century BCE Jewish philosopher Philo was profoundly affected by Hellenism: the

*Below Painting of the Temple of Solomon from the Hellenistic Dura-Europos synagogue in Syria, 3rd century CE.*

## RABBINIC JUDAISM AND HELLENISM

With regard to the rabbis, a number of tales are told about Hillel, which recall Socratic and Cynic anecdotes. Further, Joshua ben Hananiah's discussions with the Athenian, Alexandrian and Roman philosophers, Meir's disputations with the Cynic Oenomaus of Gadara, and Yehuda Ha-Nasi's discussions with Antoninus illustrate rabbinic interest. Platonism appears to have influenced the rabbis with its theory of ideas. In addition, there are a number of parallels between the Epicureans and the rabbis. The Stoic ideal of the sage as well as the Stoic technique of allegorizing the law appear to have influenced Philo. Possibly the rules for the administration of the Essenes were influenced by Pythagoreanism – Josephus in any case observed that the Essenes followed the Pythagorean way of life.

*Above Menelaus became high priest after bribing Antiochus IV with tribute money. 13th-century French illustration.*

influence of Greek thought transcends mere language and affected his entire philosophical system.

## ART AND LITERATURE

Beyond literary works, Greek influence is clearly illustrated in Hellenistic Jewish art and architecture. According to Josephus (37/38–100CE), the courts and colonnades of the Temple built by Herod in Jerusalem were in the Greek style. In synagogues in Palestine and the Diaspora, especially at Dura-Europos in Mesopotamia, the artwork was in direct violation of biblical and rabbinic prohibitions. The symbols used represent a kind of allegorization through art, similar to what Philo had attempted through philosophy. There is even evidence that some Jews adopted pagan elements in the charms and amulets they created. It is not surprising therefore that contact with Hellenism produced deviations from the Jewish tradition. Writers and artists who used extreme allegories in their work interpreted ceremonial laws as only a parable. Others relaxed their Jewish observance in order to become citizens of Alexandria. Indeed, the city of Alexandria, where Hellenism was most manifest, was

the only place where Christianity seems to have made real inroads in converting Jews.

## JEWISH RESISTANCE

The spread of Hellenism gave rise to powerful resistance among the observant. Jewish struggle against Greek and Roman domination was provoked by a reaction to what was seen as spiritual corruption. Jewish monotheism and observance of the covenant were challenged by the influence of foreign ideas. This was most manifest in the Hasmonean revolt. When Antiochus IV conquered Jerusalem in 167BCE, he banned circumcision, Sabbath observance and the reading

of the Torah; he also decreed that the Temple should be dedicated to the worship of the Greek god Zeus, that pigs should be sacrificed on the altar, and that all people, including non-Jews, should be allowed to worship there. In championing Hellenism, he underestimated Jewish resistance to such reforms. Many Jews were prepared to die rather than violate their traditions, and in the end the nation triumphed against its oppressors.

*Below Seleucid general Nicanor attacked the Palestinian rebel leader Judah ha-Maccabee and the Jews on the Sabbath, during the Hasmonean revolt. Drawing by Gustave Doré, 1865.*

# SAMARITANS

IN THE NORTHERN KINGDOM THE SAMARITANS KEPT THEIR OWN
TRADITIONS BASED ON SCRIPTURE. AS TIME PASSED, HOSTILITY GREW
BETWEEN THE JEWISH AND THE SAMARITAN PEOPLES.

In ancient times the Samaritans constituted a separate people originating from within the Jewish community. This Jewish sect, which occupied Samaria after the conquest of the Northern Kingdom by the Assyrians, developed its own interpretation of the faith. Intermingling with the resident non-Jewish population, its mixed community continued to follow the Jewish way of life while simultaneously adopting pagan practices.

When Cyrus of Persia (590/580–529BCE) conquered Babylon in the 6th century CE, he allowed the Jews to return from Babylonia to their homeland. When the Samaritans offered to help these returning exiles rebuild the Temple, the governor of Judea Zerubbabel, who supervised the repair and restoration of the Temple, refused their offer since he regarded them as

*Below* On Passover eve, Samaritans today sacrifice a lamb, which is roasted whole and eaten by the community.

of uncertain racial origin and was suspicious of their worship. Recognizing that they would be excluded from the state which these exiles were intent on creating, the Samaritans persuaded the Persian officials responsible for the western empire that the plans for restoration were illegal, thereby delaying work on the Temple for ten years or more. This was the beginning of the enmity between the Jewish and Samaritan peoples, which continued for hundreds of years.

## BELIEF AND PRACTICE

Despite their rejection from the Jewish community, the Samaritans remained loyal to traditional belief and practice. In its earliest form, the Samaritan creed consisted of a simple belief in God and the Torah (Pentateuch). For the Samaritans, God is the wholly other – he is manifest in all things, all powerful and beyond comprehension. His purposes for Israel and all peoples were communicated to Moses

*Above* In the 1920s, arranged marriages among Samaritan children of the West Bank were still common.

on Mount Sinai. According to Samaritan tradition, Moses was God's representative who wrote the Torah and authorized Mount Gerizim as the place that God chose for sacrifice. In addition, the Samaritans subscribed to a belief in resurrection and anticipated the arrival of one who would restore all things prior to the final judgement of God.

Given that the Samaritans possessed only the Torah as the sole authoritative source, the Pentateuch served as the basis of their religious practices. Frequently the Samaritans were stricter about the interpretation of biblical law than the rabbis because of their adherence to the letter of the law. In other cases, Samaritan law deviated from rabbinic traditions because of different interpretations of the text.

Regarding the Sabbath, for example, the Samaritans held four prayer services. The first, on the Sabbath eve, lasted for about an hour before the setting of the sun. This was followed on the Sabbath morning by a second service, which began between 3 and 4 a.m. The afternoon service was held only on regular Sabbaths and those that fall during

the counting of the Omer; it began at noon and lasted for about two hours. The fourth prayer service took place at the end of the Sabbath and continued for about half an hour until the sun set.

## BELIEF AND PRACTICE

In addition to Sabbath observance, the Samaritans also celebrated the other festivals recorded in Scripture. For the Samaritan community, the Passover was of central significance. On the eve of the festival, the Samaritans carried out the sacrifice of the paschal lamb on Mount Gerizim. At twilight on the 14th day of the first month, all members of the community gathered at the site of the altar in two groups; the first carried out the sacrifice and the second engaged in prayer. The High Priest then climbed on to a large stool and gave the signal to slaughter the sheep while reading the account of the Exodus from Egypt. Then a number of sheep corresponding to the families present were slaughtered.

Another major festival is Shavuot, when the Samaritans made a pilgrimage to Mount Gerizim. This

*Below A magnificent Samaritan Torah case decorated in gold with images of objects used in the Temple.*

*Above At Shavuot, Samaritans parade at Mount Gerizim, Israel, celebrating the giving of the law on Mount Sinai.*

holiday was celebrated on the 50th day of the counting of the Omer. The period is divided into seven weeks; in each week the Samaritans devoted the Sabbath to one of the places that the children of Israel passed on the Exodus from Egypt before arriving at Mount Sinai. On the first day after the sixth Sabbath, the Samaritans celebrated the day standing on Mount Sinai – there they prayed and read from the Torah (Pentateuch) from the middle of the night until the following evening. The seventh Sabbath is called the celebration of the Ten Commandments. The pilgrimage itself began early in the evening and all places holy to the Samaritans were visited.

Turning to the literature of the Samaritan community, the earliest work was the Pentateuch, which served as the centre of Samaritan life. The *Defter* constituted the oldest part of the liturgy and was probably written in the 4th century CE. There were also Samaritan chronicles, including the *Asatir*, a midrashic work, and *Al-Tolidah*, which contained various genealogical lists. The Samaritan Book of Joshua recounted the history of the Samaritan people from the initiation of Joshua to the days of Baba Rabbah. The *Annals* by Abu al-Fath were composed in the 14th century and were explained in the 19th to 20th centuries by Jacob

ben Harun. The *New Chronicle* was written in Samaritan Hebrew by Av-Sakhva ben Asad ha-Danfi and related events from Adam to 1900CE. The Samaritan corpus included a variety of halakhic works, Pentaetuch commentaries, and grammatical studies.

In all cases, Samaritan literature was centred around the Pentateuch and the religious life of the community. The purpose of these works was to guide the community in understanding the meaning of Scripture, ensuring that the biblical precepts were fulfilled in the lives of the adherents. This religious orientation illustrates the traditionalism of the Samaritan sect despite its deviation from mainstream Judaism. Holding fast to the religious tenets of the faith, the Samaritans strictly adhered to the Jewish way of life as they understood it. In this respect they regarded themselves as following an authentic form of Judaism despite their divergence from the rabbis.

Throughout its history the Samaritan community was committed to observing the law and fulfilling its covenant duties as it understood them.

*Below A Samaritan priest with the ancient Pentateuch in the Samaritan synagogue in Nablus, West Bank.*

# SADDUCEES

MEMBERS OF A 2ND-CENTURY BCE JEWISH SECT, POSSIBLY FORMED AS A POLITICAL PARTY, THE SADDUCEES BELIEVED THE TORAH WAS DIVINELY REVEALED AND BIBLICAL LAW MUST BE STRICTLY FOLLOWED.

According to tradition, the Sadducees were followers of the teachings of the High Priest Zadok. Scholars, however, have pointed out that this explanation is unlikely since the Sadducees made their debut in history as supporters of the Hasmonean high priests. Thus, the term 'Sadducees' may be a Hebraization of the Greek word *sundikoi*, or 'members of the council'. This would mark them out as councillors of the Hasmoneans even though they themselves came to associate their name with the Hebrew *zedek*, or 'righteous'. According to rabbinic sources, the Sadducees were not named after the High Priest Zadok, but rather

*Below A fanciful 19th-century lithograph showing the breastplate and supposed costume of the Jewish high priest.*

*Right Jewish historian Flavius Josephus, who described the Hasmonean revolt, is brought before Titus, Roman commander in Judea during the Jewish revolt 66CE.*

another Zadok who rebelled against the teachings of Antigonus of Soko, a government official of Judea in the 3rd century BCE who was a predecessor of the rabbis.

Despite these different interpretations, it is clear that the Sadducees were a priestly group, associated with the leadership of the Jerusalem Temple. Possibly, the Sadducees belonged to the aristocratic clan of the Hasmonean high priests who replaced the previous high priestly lineage that permitted the Syrian Emperor Antiochus IV Epiphanes to desecrate the Temple of Jerusalem with idolatrous sacrifices. The festival of Hanukkah celebrates the overthrowing of the Syrian forces, the re-dedication of the Temple, and the instalment of a new Hasmonean priestly line.

In the following years the Hasmoneans ruled as priest-kings; like other aristocracies across the Hellenistic world, they were increasingly influenced by Hellenistic ideas. Like the Epicureans, the Sadducees rejected the existence of an afterlife, thereby denying the Pharisaic doctrine of the resurrection of the dead. The Dead Sea Scrolls community – identified with the Essenes – were led by a high priestly caste who were believed to be the descendants of the legitimate high priestly lineage which the Hasmoneans removed. According to the Dead Sea Scrolls, the current high priests were interlopers since the Hasmoneans constituted a different priestly line.

## THE INTERPRETATION OF SCRIPTURE

Most of what is known about the Sadducees is derived from the writings of the Jewish historian Josephus; other information is contained in the Talmud. According to these sources, the Sadducees rejected the Pharisaic belief in an oral Torah. Instead, they interpreted the Torah literally. In their personal lives this led to an excessively stringent lifestyle.

The fact that the Sadducees had a high opinion of the Five Books of Moses does not mean that they denied that the other books of the Bible – the prophets and historical writings – were divinely inspired. Yet they refused to accept the other biblical books as sources of law. When a Sadducee had to judge a case he would look in the written Torah and ignore the oral traditions that the Pharisees accepted as normative. One of the consequences of such an approach was that the Sadducees stressed the importance of the priests in the Temple cult, while the Pharisees insisted on the participation of all Jews.

In developing their approach to Scripture, the Sadducees had interpretative traditions of their own which were written down in a

*Above Ceremonies at the Temple in Jerusalem, from the Bible Mozarabe, a 10th-century Spanish manuscript.*

book of jurisprudence known as the Book of Decrees. The existence of this code is known from a rabbinical source, the *Megilla Ta'anit*, a calendar-like text, which states that the Book of Decrees was revoked on the 4th of Tammuz, although no year is given. The code that is described is very harsh. An example of the

*Below A section of the oldest surviving map of the Holy Land. This part of the 5th-century CE mosaic map from Madaba, Jordan, shows Jerusalem and the area around.*

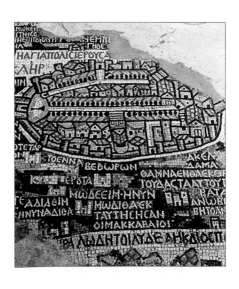

Sadducean approach concerns the interpretation of the biblical law concerning 'an eye for an eye.' The Pharisees believed that the value of an eye was to be sought by the perpetrator of its loss rather than actually removing his eye in accordance with the law. The Sadducees, however, insisted that the law should be taken literally.

## SADDUCEAN THEOLOGY

Regarding Sadducean belief, many sources stress that the Sadducees believed that souls die with their bodies. The rabbinical text known as *Avot de Rabbi Nathan* states that a discussion about this subject was the cause of the schism between the Sadducees and the Pharisees.

According to the *Avot de Rabbi Nathan*, the Pharisee teacher Antigonus of Soko had two disciples who used to study his words. They taught them to their disciples, and their disciples to their disciples. These proceeded to examine the words closely and demanded, 'Why did our ancestors see fit to say this thing? Is it possible that a labourer should do his work all day and not take his reward in the evening? If our ancestors, forsooth, had known that there is no other world and that there will be a resurrection of the dead, they would not have spoken in this manner.'

So they arose and withdrew from the study of the oral Torah, and split into two sects.

## TEMPLE PRACTICES

With regard to Temple ritual, the Sadducees insisted that the daily burnt sacrifices were to be offered by the high priest at his own expense, whereas the Pharisees maintained that they were to be furnished as a national sacrifice at the cost of the Temple treasury. The Sadducees also held that the meal offering belonged to the priest's portion, whereas the Pharisees claimed

*Above A 15th-century miniature showing that ritual animal slaughter is a part of the Jewish way of life.*

it was for the altar. The Sadducees insisted on a high degree of purity in those who officiated at the preparation of the ashes of the Red Heifer. By contrast, the Pharisees opposed such strictness.

With regard to the kindling of the incense in the vessel with which the high priest entered the Holy of Holies on the Day of Atonement, the Sadducees claimed it should take place outside so that he might be wrapped in smoke while meeting the Shekhinah (divine presence) within; the Pharisees insisted that the incense be kindled inside.

In addition, the Sadducees opposed the popular festivity of the water libation and the procession that preceded it on each night of Sukkot, marking the end of the agricultural year. They also opposed the Pharisaic assertion that the scrolls of the Torah have the power to render ritually unclean the hands that touch them; the Pharisaic idea of the *eruv* (the merging of several private precincts into one so that food and vessels can be carried from place to place); and the formula introduced by the Pharisees in divorce documents.

# PHARISEES

ALONGSIDE THE SADDUCEES AND THE ESSENES, THE PHARISEES CONSTITUTED A MAJOR JEWISH PARTY IN THE HELLENISTIC PERIOD. AFTER THE FALL OF THE TEMPLE, THE PHARISEES DOMINATED JEWISH LIFE.

The Pharisees were a Jewish religious and political party who emerged shortly after the Hasmonean revolt in about 165–160BCE. In all likelihood they were the successors of the Hasideans who had promoted the observance of Jewish ritual and the study of the Torah. Regarding themselves as followers of Ezra, they maintained the validity of the Oral Torah as well as of the Written Torah.

## THE EMERGENCE OF THE PHARISEES

The origin of their name is uncertain, though it is generally believed that the name Pharisees derives from the word *parash*, or 'to be separated' – thus Pharisees would mean the

separated ones or the separatists. Determined to adapt biblical law to new conditions, they formulated a complex system of scriptural interpretation. Initially the Pharisees were small in number, but by the 1st century CE they had profoundly influenced the religious beliefs, practices and social attitudes of the majority of the nation.

The Pharisees' first bid for power took place in a period two centuries after the Babylonian exile, during the struggle to remove the Temple and religious control from the leadership of the Sadducees. The inception of synagogue worship was an attempt by the Pharisees to undermine the privileged authority of the Sadducees; in addition, ceremonies that were originally part of the Temple cult were carried over to the home, and scholars of non-priestly descent came to play an important role in national affairs. Unlike the Sadducees,

*Above The prophet Ezra reads the law, which was expanded by the Pharisees. A 2nd-century CE painting from Dura-Europos synagogue, Syria.*

the Pharisees believed that the Written Torah required expansion. As a consequence, Phari-saic sages developed an elaborate system of biblical interpretation.

## PHARISAIC SCHOLARSHIP

According to rabbinic writings, Pharisaic sages first appeared as the men of the Great Assembly. Subsequently there were five generations of *zugot* (pairs) of outstanding Pharisees who served as leaders of the Pharisaic supreme court until the beginning of the 1st century CE. During the civil war of the reign of Alexander Janneus, the Pharisees were among the king's enemies. Later they were restored by Salome Alexandra. The Pharisees then exacted retribution on the Sadducees. The Jewish historian

*Below Jesus on trial before the Sanhedrin, the Jewish supreme court, which was dominated by the Sadducees. A 6th-century CE mosaic from Ravenna.*

Josephus records there were about 6,000 Pharisees during King Herod's reign. By the second or third decades of the 1st century CE, the Pharisees had become divided into two schools of thought: the school of Hillel and the school of Shammai.

While scholars disagree on whether the Pharisees were the dominant group in Erez Israel before 70CE, there is no doubt that once the Temple in Jerusalem was destroyed by the Romans they became the leading party. As such, the Pharisees exerted a profound influence on Jewish life. The hereditary priestly caste was superseded by a new form of leadership that was based on learning, knowledge and wisdom. The most important relationship among the Pharisees was between a teacher and student. A sage's reputation was based on learning transmitted orally from him to his students. Pharisaic maxims from this period deal with such ethical issues as honesty in judging, ethical responsibility and serving God.

## THE DEVELOPMENT OF PHARISAIC JUDAISM

Towards the end of the 1st century CE under Rabban Gamaliel II, the Sanhedrin (rabbinical assembly) at Yavneh strengthened a post-Temple form of Judaism. The term rabbi came into general use for a sage recognized as such by his peers. The sages at Yavneh summarized the

*Above Giacomo Giaquerio's shifty painting of a Pharisee from a 15th-century north Italian fresco about the life of Jesus, at the Castello della Manta.*

teachings of the earlier schools of Hillel and Shammai. In addition, they canonized the Scriptures, gave a more precise form to daily prayer, and transferred to the synagogue and the Sanhedrin various observances associated with the Temple. An ordination procedure for rabbis was instituted and the Sanhedrin exerted control over all aspects of Jewish life.

As far as the belief system of the Pharisees was concerned, Pharisaic theology was based on the conviction that God is an omnipotent, spiritual being who is all-wise, all-knowing and all-merciful. God, they believed, loves all his creatures and expects human beings to act justly and compassionately. Although God is omniscient and omnipotent, he endowed human beings with the power to choose between good and evil. Every person, the Pharisees stressed, has two impulses: the *yetzer tov* (good inclination) and the *yetzer ha-ra* (evil

*Left This floor mosaic from an ancient synagogue in Jericho shows a menorah above the inscription 'Shalom al Israel' (Peace upon Israel').*

inclination). Yet despite the belief in free will, the Pharisees held that everything in the world was ordained by God. Unlike the Sadducees, Pharisees believed in the resurrection of the dead. This concept of a future life made possible the belief in the divine justice in the face of calamity and suffering.

Pharisaic theological reflection is found in various collections of midrashim (commentaries on Scripture). Unlike the Mishnah, which consists of legislation presented without explicit reference to Scriptural sources, rabbinic aggadah (commentary on the Bible) focuses on the contemporary relevance of specific texts. Though the sages were not speculative philosophers, they expressed their religious views in these works and attempted to apply this teaching to daily life. These midrashic sources, along with the aggadic sections of the Talmud, serve as the basis for reconstructing the theology of early rabbinic Judaism.

*Below A 15th-century German Torah scroll. Unlike the Sadducees, the Pharisees believed the Written Torah needed expansion.*

# ESSENES

THE ESSENES WERE THE THIRD PRINCIPAL SECT IN THE HELLENISTIC PERIOD. CONGREGATED IN SEMI-MONASTIC COMMUNITIES, THEY SAW THE HELLENIZERS AND SADDUCEES AS VIOLATORS OF GOD'S LAW.

The dispute between the Pharisees and the Sadducees centred around the religious leadership of the Jewish people. However, there were other smaller groupings that withdrew from society into holy communities who rejected the priests who controlled the Temple. Pre-eminent among these groups were the Essenes, who, according to the Jewish historian Josephus (37/38–100CE), believed in fate and the immortality of the soul. They lived as a separatist association in the towns of Judea and also in rural communes, where members engaged in agricultural and artisan labour as well as the study of religious writings.

Admission to this order occurred only after several periods of probation and preparation. Those initiated

*Below A ritual bath or* mikveh *of the Essene sect at Qumran, 2nd century* BCE. *Water in* mikvehs *should come from natural springs or rivers.*

into the faith had to swear obedience to the rules and leadership of the community and promise that they would keep secret its special doctrines. Discipline was enforced by the expulsion of lax members after a vote by the council. Among the inner circle, property was owned jointly. Food, clothing and other necessities were administered by overseers. Essene rituals included wearing white garments, taking frequent ritual baths and eating community meals accompanied by prayer and a reading from Scripture.

According to Josephus, the Essenes numbered about 4,000 in the 1st century CE. He asserted that Essene prophets were held in high regard by the masses and the kings for the accuracy of their predictions and medical knowledge.

### THE DEAD SEA SECT

According to modern scholars, an Essene-like group lived between 150BCE and 68CE in the Judean desert near the Dead Sea. In 1947 Arab shepherds discovered a group of documents – the Dead Sea Scrolls – which were traced to 11 caves not far from Jerusalem where they were preserved by the desert climate. The Dead Sea Scrolls include communal rule books, hymns and biblical commentaries. Near this site was uncovered the remains of a community that flourished from about 130BCE to the time of the Roman–Jewish war. The ruins discovered on a cliff north of the Wadi Qumran include a tower, assembly chamber, kitchen, writing room and worship space. It appears that the members of this sect slept in tents, caves or upper rooms of this building.

*Above El Greco's 16th-century painting of John the Baptist, cousin of Jesus, who may have had contact with the Essenes.*

An elaborate system of cisterns ensured an adequate supply of water for the members of this group. The community's cemetery contained a thousand burials. For nearly two centuries, Qumran was the headquarters of a well-organized settlement,

*Below This fragment of the Dead Sea Scrolls shows the Song of Degrees, one of the Psalms of King David.*

*Right The Qumran caves in the Judean desert, where the Dead Sea Scrolls were discovered 1946–56.*

which at its height numbered about 200. The Dead Sea Scrolls were most likely the remains of the Qumran library, which was hidden during the Roman–Jewish war when Qumran was destroyed by the Romans.

## QUMRAN AND THE ESSENES

Assuming that Qumran was an Essene community and the Dead Sea Scrolls a collection of their writings, then the movement was both quietistic and philosophical. The scrolls depict a priest-dominated group who viewed the Temple as dominated by corrupt men who had usurped power.

From references in Qumran texts, the site seems to have been founded by a priestly 'Teacher of Righteousness', who was persecuted as a wicked priest. The community regarded the *Kittim* (possibly the Romans) with hostility and regarded itself as the true heir of the Mosaic covenant and of God's promises. Members of the order had been preserved from the domination of evil powers. The group had been saved from the domination of these forces in order to settle in the wilderness

under the leadership of true priests, until they could return to a Temple that had been purified.

As members of the covenant, these individuals constituted the divine elect of God, who had predetermined whether they would join the holy community (Sons of Light) or remain outside with those hostile to God (Sons of Darkness). Eventually the Sons of Light would issue forth in ritual combat under the leadership of their divinely appointed leaders to re-establish the remnant of Israel in the Promised Land and to witness the victory of God over the entire earth.

### INDIVIDUAL CHARISMATICS

In the Judean desert there were also individual charismatics who, though not formally affiliated with the Essenes, adopted similar attitudes and practices. John the Baptist, for example, was described in the New Testament as clothed with camel's hair, a leather girdle around his waist, and eating locusts and wild honey. According to Scripture, he preached a baptism of repentance for the forgiveness of sins. Another figure was John's mentor, Bannus. According to the Jewish historian Josephus, Bannus dwelt in the wilderness, wearing only such clothing as trees provided, feeding on such things as grew of themselves and using frequent ablutions of cold water, by day and night for purity's sake. In the 40s of the 1st century CE, Theudas declared himself a prophet and persuaded crowds to follow him to the River Jordan. A decade later an Egyptian prophet led his group to the Mount of Olives outside Jerusalem, proposing to force his way into the city, overpower the Roman garrison and set himself up as ruler of the people.

# CHAPTER 2

# RABBINIC JUDAISM

From the 1st century BCE to the 2nd century CE, rabbinic scholars engaged in the interpretation of Scripture. In their view, the Five Books of Moses were given by God to Moses on Mount Sinai. This belief implies that God is the direct source of all laws recorded in the Torah, and is also indirectly responsible for the authoritative legal judgements of the rabbis. Alongside their exegesis of biblical law, scholars also produced interpretations of Scripture in rabbinic commentaries and the Talmud. Within these texts is a wealth of theological, philosophical and mystical speculation.

The Karaites, a radical sect, later challenged rabbinic Judaism. Their guiding interpretative principle was: 'Search thoroughly in Scripture and do not rely on my opinion.' Further challenges were posed by the Shabbateans and Frankists. In the 17th century, a self-proclaimed messianic king, Shabbetai Tzvi, electrified the Jewish world with his claims. After his conversion to Islam, the majority of his followers were despondent, yet a number continued to believe in his messiahship. These Shabbateans and a later Shabbatean sect, the Frankists, remained convinced that the messianic era had begun.

*Opposite The title page of a Hebrew manuscript of the* Guide for the Perplexed
*by the 12th-century Jewish philosopher and rabbinic scholar Moses Maimonides.*

*Above In 1999, Menachem Joskowicz, Chief Rabbi of Poland, asked John-Paul II
to remove a large Christian cross from land bordering the concentration camp of Auschwitz.*

# PHARISAIC JUDAISM

THE RABBIS CONSTITUTED A SCHOLARLY CLASS DRAWN FROM THE PHARISEES. THEY PRODUCED A MASSIVE CORPUS OF LEGAL TEXTS, BIBLICAL EXEGESIS, THEOLOGICAL WORKS AND ETHICAL REFLECTIONS.

With the destruction of the Second Temple in 70CE, the Pharisees emerged as the dominant religious group. These sages were determined to forge a new form of Judaism based on scriptural precedent. In their view, both the written and the oral Torah were expressions of God's will.

### RABBINIC LAW
During the Tannaitic period (1st century BCE–2nd century CE) and the Amoraic period (2nd–6th century CE) rabbinic scholars – referred to as the Tannaim and the Amoraim respectively – actively engaged in the interpretation of Scripture. According to the Pharisaic tradition, both the written Torah and its interpretation (oral Torah) were given by God to Moses on Mount Sinai. This belief, which implies that God is the

*Below Moses ben Yekuthiel Hakohen commissioned what is now known as* The Rothschild Miscellany *in 1479 to show customs of religious and secular life as expounded by rabbinic sages in a Jewish Renaissance household.*

direct source of all laws recorded in the Pentateuch and indirectly responsible for the authoritative legal judgements of the rabbis, served as the justification for the rabbinic exposition of scriptural ordinances.

### INTERPRETING SCRIPTURE
Alongside the halakha, or the 'exegesis of Jewish law', scholars also produced aggadah, or 'interpretations of Scripture in which new meanings of the text were expounded' in midrashim or 'rabbinic commentaries', and in the Talmud. Within the aggadic texts is found a wealth of theological speculation about such topics as the nature of God, divine justice, the coming of the Messiah and the hereafter. In addition, ethical considerations were of considerable importance in the discussions of these teachers of the faith.

Early rabbinic Judaism thus covered a wide variety of areas that were all embraced by the holy word revealed on Mount Sinai, and this literature served as the foundation of later Judaism as it developed through the centuries.

*Above Sage and pupil learning Hillel's golden rule –'What is hateful to you, do not do to another'. From the Coburg Pentateuch by Samuel Halevi, 1395.*

### RABBINIC EXEGESIS
The exegesis found in rabbinic literature of the Tannaitic and Amoraic periods is largely of two types: direct and explicit exegesis where the biblical text is commented on or accompanied by a remark, and indirect exegesis where a scriptural text is cited to support an assertion. In the case of direct exegesis, the rabbis frequently reinforced their exhortations by a biblical sentence which expressed their sentiments. It was also a usual custom in rabbinic circles to cite a text and then draw out its meaning. Further, the rabbis frequently stressed that a word should be understood in its strictest sense. Occasionally they also employed typological exegesis to explain the meaning of Scripture.

Turning to the method of indirect exegesis, it was a common practice in rabbinic literature to draw deductions from scriptural texts by means of a number of formal hermeneutical rules. Hillel the elder, who flourished about a century before the destruction of the Second Temple, is reported to have been the first to lay down these principles. In the 2nd century CE Ishmael ben Elisha expanded Hillel's seven

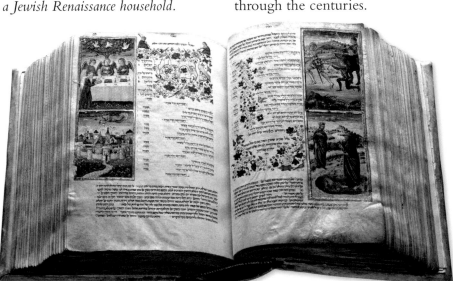

*Above A rabbi reads to his people from a* Sefer Torah*, the handwritten copy of the Pentateuch. From the 14th-century Barcelona Haggadah.*

rules into thirteen by sub-dividing them, omitting one, and adding a new one of his own.

These various methods of excgesis were based on the deeply held conviction that the Bible is sacred, that it is susceptible of interpretation and that, when properly understood, it will guide the life of the worthy. By means of this process of explanation of God's revelation, rabbinic

*Below Rabbinic study group at Bircas Hatorah in Jerusalem, 1994, a yeshiva which is dedicated to Torah education.*

authorities were able to infuse the tradition with new meaning and renewed relevance.

## RABBINIC THEOLOGY

Unlike the Mishnah, which consists of legislation presented without explicit reference to a Scriptural source, rabbinic aggadah focuses on the contemporary relevance of specific biblical texts. The early halakhic midrashim consists of Tannaitic commentaries on the legal verses of the Bible. Narrative midrashim, on the other hand, derive from sermons given by the Amoraim in synagogues and academies. Within these texts the rabbis propounded their theological views by means of stories, legends, parables and maxims based on Scripture. Within aggadic sources, the rabbis expressed their profound reflections on human life and God's nature and activity in the world. Unlike the legal precepts of the Torah and the rabbinic expansion of these scriptural ordinances, these theological opinions were not binding on the Jewish community. They were formulated instead to educate, inspire and edify those to whom they were addressed. Study of the Torah was a labour of love that had no end, a task whose goal was to serve the will of God.

*Above A contemporary North African rabbi wearing Arab-style headgear and clothing and studying a Hebrew book.*

## RABBINIC ETHICS

Supplementing these theological reflections, the rabbis in midrashic and talmudic sources also encouraged the Jewish people to put the teachings of the law into effect in their everyday lives. In their view the kingdom of God is inconsistent with injustice and social misery – the effort to bring about the perfection of the world so that God will reign in majesty is the responsibility of every Jew. Jewish ethics as enshrined in rabbinic literature were inextricably related to the coming of God's Kingdom. Throughout rabbinic sources, Jews were encouraged to strive for the highest conception of life, in which the rule of truth, righteousness and holiness will be established among humankind. Such a desire is the eternal hope of God's people – a longing for God's Kingdom. The coming of his rule requires a struggle for the reign of justice and righteousness on earth. This Kingdom is not an internalized, spiritualized, other-worldly concept, rather it involves human activity in a historical context.

# EARLY MYSTICAL JUDAISM

ALONGSIDE OTHER MODES OF SCRIPTURAL INTERPRETATION, RAB-
BINIC SCHOLARS ENGAGED IN MYSTICAL EXEGESIS. THEY FORMULATED
COSMOLOGICAL THEORIES AS WELL AS METHODS OF HEAVENLY ASCENT.

Within aggadic sources, the rabbis also engaged in mystical speculation. These doctrines were often of a secret nature; in a midrash on Genesis it is reported that these mystical traditions were repeated in a whisper so that they would not be overheard by those for whom they were not intended. These secret doctrines served as the basis for the evolution of a mystical form of the Jewish tradition.

## THE DIVINE CHARIOT

In the rabbis' mystical reflections, the first chapter of Ezekiel played an important role. In this biblical text the *merkavah*, or 'divine chariot', is described in detail, and this scriptural source served as the basis for rabbinic speculation about the nature of the deity. It was the aim of the mystic to be a 'merkavah rider' so

*Below God creating the earth, planets and stars, from a 15th-century Armenian* Sefer Yezirah *or 'Book of Creation'.*

*Right The Vision of Ezekiel from a 15th-century Bible, showing the winged symbols of the four Christian evangelists – a man, a lion, an ox and an eagle.*

that he would be able to penetrate the heavenly mysteries. Within this contemplative system, the rabbis believed that the pious could free themselves from the fetters of bodily existence and enter paradise. A further dimension of this theory is that certain pious individuals can temporarily ascend into the unseen realm and, having learnt the deepest secrets, may return to earth. These mystics were able to attain a state of ecstasy, to behold visions and hear voices. As students of the merkavah they were the ones to attain the highest degree of spiritual insight.

## THE MYSTICS AND CREATION

Closely associated with this form of speculation were *Maaseh Bereshit*, or 'mystical theories about creation'. Within aggadic sources the rabbis discussed the hidden meanings of the Genesis narrative. The most important early treatise, possibly from the 2nd century CE, which describes the process of creation is *Sefer Yezirah*, or 'Book of Creation'. According to this cosmological text, God created the universe by 32 mysterious paths consisting of 22 letters of the Hebrew alphabet together with ten *sefirot*, or 'emanations'. Concerning these 22 letters, the *Sefer Yezirah* states: 'He hewed them, combined them, weighed them, interchanged them and through them produced the whole creation and everything that is destined to come into being.'

## DIVINE EMANATION

These recondite doctrines were supplemented by a theory of divine emanation. The first of the sefirot is the spirit of the living God; the second is air and is derived from the first – on it are hewn the 22 letters. The third sefirah is the water that comes from the air; the fourth is the fire that comes from water through which God made the heavenly wheels, the seraphim and the ministering angels. The remaining six sefirot are the six dimensions of space – north, south, east, west, height and depth.

These ten sefirot are the moulds into which all created things were originally cast. They constitute form

---

**HEAVENLY HALLS**

A description of the experiences of these merkavah mystics is contained in *hekhalot*, or 'heavenly hall', literature from the later Gaonic period (from the 7th to the 11th century CE). In order to make their heavenly ascent, these mystics followed strict ascetic disciplines, including fasting, ablution and the invocation of God's name. After reaching a state of ecstasy, the mystic was able to enter the seven heavenly halls and attain a vision of the divine chariot.

rather than matter. The 22 letters are the prime cause of matter: everything that exists is due to the creative force of the Hebrew letters, but they receive their form from the sefirot. According to this, God transcends the universe; nothing exists outside him. The visible world is the result of the emanations of the divine. God is the cause of the form and matter of the cosmos. By combining emanation and creation, the *Sefer Yezirah* tries to harmonize the concept of divine imminence and transcendence. God is imminent in that the sefirot are an outpouring of his spirit. He is transcendent in that the matter, which was shaped into the forms, is the product of his creative action.

## MEDIEVAL MYSTICISM

Drawing on these ideas, early medieval Jewish mystics elaborated a complex system of mystical thought. Referring to the traditions of early rabbinic mysticism, writers expanded and elaborated many of the doctrines found in midrashic and talmudic sources as well as in the *Sefer Yezirah*. In their writings these mystics saw themselves as the transmitters of a

*Below A medieval Jewish hamsa, sometimes known as the hand of Miriam. Amulets like this were used to protect people from evil spirits.*

secret tradition which describes the supernal world to which all human beings are linked. One strand of this heritage focused on the nature of the spiritual world and its relationship with the terrestrial plane. The other more practical side attempted to use energies from the spiritual world to bring about miracle-working effects. According to these mystics, all of creation is in a struggle for redemption and liberation from evil, and their goal was to restore world harmony so that universal salvation would be attained through the coming of the Messiah and the establishment of the Kingdom of God.

Pre-eminent among these early medieval mystics were Jewish settlers in the Rhineland, the Hasidei Ashkenaz. Among the greatest figures

*Above This 19th-century Russian icon shows the prophet Elijah contemplating his ascent to heaven in a fiery chariot. Jewish mystics saw themselves as chariot riders on an ascent towards the Divine.*

of this period were the 12th-century Samuel ben Kalonymus of Speyer, his son Judah ben Samuel of Regensburg, and Eleazar ben Judah of Worms, who composed the treatise *The Secret of Secrets*. In their writings these mystics were preoccupied with the mystery of divine unity. God himself, they believed, cannot be known by human reason. The aim of the Hasidei Ashkenaz was to attain a vision of God's glory through the cultivation of the life of piety, which embraced devotion, saintliness and contemplation.

# KABBALISTIC JUDAISM

MEDIEVAL MYSTICS, KNOWN AS KABBALISTS, CONTINUED THE TRADITIONS OF EARLIER THINKERS. THE AIM OF THE KABBALISTS WAS TO ATTAIN THE HIGHEST LEVELS OF SPIRITUAL ILLUMINATION.

Parallel with the emergence of the Hasidei Ashkenaz, Jewish Kabbalists in southern France engaged in speculation about the nature of God, the existence of evil and the religious life. In 12th-century Provence the earliest Kabbalistic text, the *Bahir*, reinterpreted the concept of the sefirot as depicted in the *Sefer Yezirah*. According to the *Bahir*, the sefirot are conceived as vessels, crowns or words that constitute the structure of the divine realm.

Basing themselves on this work, various Provence Jews engaged in similar mystical reflection. Isaac the Blind conceived of the sefirot as emanations of a hidden dimension of the Godhead. Using neo-Platonic

*Below A Hebrew book in the garden of the Nahmamid Institute, housed in a former synagogue in Gerona, Spain, once a centre of Jewish Kabbalah.*

ideas, he argued that out of the *En Sof*, or 'infinite', emanated the first supernal essence (divine thought) from which came the remaining sefirot.

## KABBALISTS IN GERONA
In Gerona, the traditions from Isaac the Blind were broadly disseminated. One of the most important was Azriel ben Menahem who replaced divine thought with the divine will as the first emanation of the En Sof. The most famous figure of this circle was Nahmanides (1194–1270CE) who helped this mystical school gain general acceptance. In his commentary on the Torah he frequently referred to Kabbalistic notions to explain the true meaning of the text. During the time these Geronese writers were propounding their Kabbalistic theories, other mystical schools of thought developed in Spain. Influenced by the Hasidei Ashkenaz and the Sufi traditions of Islam, Abraham ben Samuel Abulafia wrote meditative texts concerning the technique of combining the letters of the alphabet as a means of realizing human aspirations toward prophecy. They developed a complex system of mystical speculation coupled with mystical practice.

## SPANISH KABBALISTS
Other Spanish Kabbalists were more attracted to Gnostic ideas. Isaac ha-Kohen elaborated the theory of a demonic emanation. The mingling of such Gnostic teaching with the Kabbalah of Gerona resulted in the major mystical work of Spanish Jewry, the Zohar, composed by Moses ben Shem Tov de Leon in Guadalajara. The author places the work in a 2nd-century CE setting, focusing on

*Above A Kabbalist at festivities in Meron, Israel, to celebrate Simeon ben Yohai, commemorated in the Zohar.*

Simeon ben Yohai and his disciples, but the doctrines of the Zohar are of a much later origin. Written in Aramaic, the text is largely a midrash in which the Torah is given a mystical or ethical interpretation.

## THE EN SOF
According to these various Kabbalistic systems, God in himself lies beyond any speculative comprehension. To express the unknowable aspect of the Divine, the early Kabbalists of both Provence and Spain referred to the Divine Infinite as En Sof – the absolute perfection in which there is no distinction or plurality. The En Sof does not reveal itself; it is beyond all thought and at times is identified with the Aristotelian First Cause. In Kabbalistic teaching, creation is bound up with the manifestation of the hidden God and his outward movement.

## DIVINE EMANATION
These sefirot emanate successively from above to below, each one revealing a stage in the process. The common order of the sefirot and the names most generally used are: (1) supreme crown; (2) wisdom; (3)

intelligence; (4) greatness; (5) power (or judgement); (6) beauty (or compassion); (7) endurance; (8) majesty; (9) foundation (or righteous one); (10) kingdom.

These ten sefirot are formally arranged in threes. The first triad consists of the first three sefirot and constitutes the intellectual realm of the inner structure of the Divine. The second triad is composed of the next three sefirot from the psychic or moral level of the Godhead. Finally, sefirot 7, 8 and 9 represent the archetypes of certain forces in nature. The remaining sefirah, kingdom, constitutes the channel between the higher and the lower worlds. The ten sefirot together demonstrate how an infinite undivided and unknowable God is the cause of all the modes of existence in the finite plane.

## SPIRITUAL REALITY

In explaining this picture of Divine creation, Kabbalists adopted a neo-Platonic conception of a ladder of spiritual reality composed of four worlds in descending order. First is the domain of Atzilut, or 'emanation', consisting of the ten sefirot which form Adam Kadmon, or 'primordial man'. The second world, based on hekhalot, or 'heavenly hall', literature, is the realm of Beriyah, or 'creation', which is made up of the throne of glory and the seven heavenly palaces. In the third world, Yezirah, or 'formation', most of the angels dwell, presided over by the angel Metatron. This is the scene of the seven heavenly halls guarded by angels to which merkavah, or 'chariot', mystics attempt to gain admission. In the fourth world of Asiyah, or 'making', are the lowest order of angels – the ophanim, who combat evil and receive prayers. This is the spiritual archetype of the material cosmos, heaven and the earthly world.

Asiyah is both the last link in the Divine chain of being and the domain where the Sitra Ahra, or 'the realm of demonic powers', is manifest; in this sphere the forces of good struggle with the demons.

## COSMIC REPAIR

For the mystic, deeds of *tikkun*, or 'cosmic repair', sustain the world, activate nature to praise God, and bring about the coupling of the tenth and the six sefirot. Such repair is accomplished by keeping the commandments which were conceived as vessels for establishing contact with the Godhead and for ensuring divine mercy. Such a religious life provided the Kabbalist with a means of integrating into the divine hierarchy of creation – the Kabbalah was able to guide the soul back to its Infinite source. The supreme rank attainable by the soul at the end of its sojourn is *devekut*, or 'mystical cleaving to God'. Devekut does not completely elim-

*Left A Kabbalistic roll of 1604 by Jacob Hebron, showing the names of God, the 10 sefirot, the 32 paths, the mystery of the letters and vowels, and the Temple.*

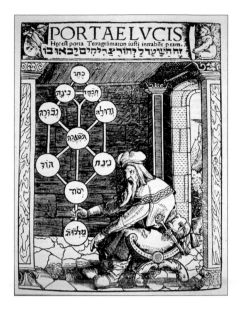

*Above German woodcut from 1516 showing a Jewish Kabbalist holding the Sefirot Tree of Life.*

inate the distance between God and human beings – it denotes instead a state of beatitude and intimate union between the soul and its source.

*Below Tree of Life Showing the Ten Spheres or sefirot, by Mark Penney Maddocks, 1976, illustrating the ten sefirot or divine emanations.*

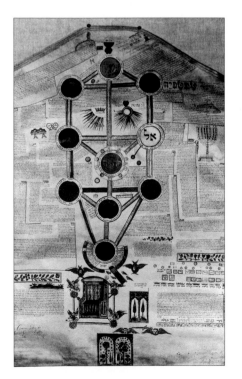

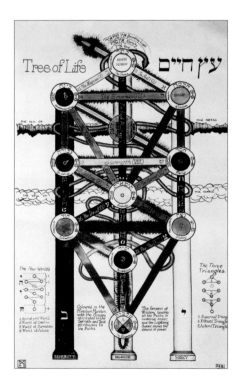

# PHILOSOPHICAL JUDAISM

JEWISH THINKERS INTERPRETED THEIR TRADITION PHILOSOPHICALLY.
THE INTERPRETATION OF THE NATURE OF GOD AND HIS ACTION
CONSTITUTED AN ALTERNATIVE CONCEPTION OF THE JEWISH FAITH.

In the Hellenistic world the Jewish philosopher Philo tried to integrate Greek philosophy and Jewish teaching into a unified whole. By applying an allegorical method of interpretation to Scripture, he explained the God of Judaism in Greek philosophical categories and reshaped Jewish notions about God, human beings and the world. Philo was the precursor of medieval Jewish philosophy which also attempted to combine alternative philosophical systems with the received biblical tradition. The beginnings of this philosophical

*Below Islamic theology had a profound impact on Jewish medieval thought. This 1237 illustration of medieval Muslim scholars is from* Maqamat *by poet and Seljuk empire government official al-Hariri of Basra (1054–1122).*

development took place in 9th-century CE Babylonia during the height of the Abbasid caliphate, when rabbinic Judaism was challenged by Karaite scholars who criticized the anthropomorphic views of God in midrashic and talmudic sources.

Added to this internal threat was the Islamic contention that Mohammed's revelation in the Koran superseded the Jewish faith. In addition, Zoroastrians and Manicheans attacked monotheism as a viable religious system. Finally, some gentile philosophers argued that the Greek scientific and philosophical world view could account for the origin of the cosmos without reference to an external deity. In combating these challenges, Jewish writers were influenced by the teachings of *kalam*, or 'Muslim

*Above This statue of Spanish poet and philosopher Solomon Ibn Gabirol stands in Malaga, where he was born in 1022.*

schools' of the 8th to the 11th century CE; in particular the contributions of one school of Muslim thought – the Mutazilite kalam – had a profound effect on Jewish thought. These Islamic scholars maintained that rational argument was vital in matters of religious belief and that Greek philosophy could serve as the handmaiden of religious faith. In their attempt to defend Judaism from internal and external assault, rabbinic authorities frequently adapted the Mutazilite kalam as an important line of defence, and as time passed they also employed other aspects of Graeco-Arabic thought in their expositions of the Jewish faith.

## SOLOMON IBN GABIROL

After the 11th century CE the Mutazilite kalam ceased to play a central role in Jewish philosophical thought. In Islam the Mutazilites were replaced by the more orthodox Asharyites, who attempted to provide a rational basis for unquestioning traditionalism. During this period the first Spanish Jewish

*Above Hebrew manuscript of 1356 of Maimonides' classic* Guide for the Perplexed. *From Huesca, Spain.*

philosopher to produce a work in the neo-Platonic tradition was Solomon Ibn Gabirol (1022–58). In his *Fountain of Life*, he argued that God and matter are not opposed as two ultimate principles – instead matter is identified with God. It emanates from the essence of the creator, forming the basis of all subsequent emanations.

## MAIMONIDES

In the following century, Moses Maimonides (1135–1204), arguably the greatest philosopher of the Middle Ages, produced *The Guide for the Perplexed*, based on Aristotelianism. Like Saadia, he addressed the question of anthropomorphic terms in the Bible. In his view, a literal reading of these passages implies that God is a corporeal being. Yet, according to Maimonides, this is a mistake. No positive attributes should be predicated of God, he argued, since the Divine is an absolute unity. Thus when God is described positively in the Bible, such ascriptions must refer to his activity. The only true attributes are

negative ones – they lead to a knowledge of God because in negation no plurality is involved.

## MAIMONIDEANS AND ANTI-MAIMONIDEANS

By the 13th century, most of the important philosophical texts of medieval thinkers had been translated into Hebrew by Jews living in southern France. This led to bitter antagonism between Maimonideans and anti-Maimonideans who believed that Maimonides had corrupted the tradition. Yet, in later centuries other philosophers emerged who continued to produce treatises grounded in Greek thought. The most prominent Jewish philosopher after Maimonides who was attracted to Aristotelianism was Gersonides (1288–1344). In his *The Wars of the*

---

### SAADIA GAON

The earliest philosopher of the medieval period was the 10th-century CE thinker, Saadia ben Joseph al-Fayyumi. As *Gaon*, or 'head', of one of the Babylonian academies, he wrote treatises on a wide range of subjects and produced the first major Jewish theological treatise of the Middle Ages, *The Book of Beliefs and Opinions*. In this study Saadia attempted to refute the religious claims of Christians, Muslims and Zoroastrians. Adapting the teaching of the Mutazilites, he argued that religious faith and reason are fully compatible. On this basis he sought to demonstrate that God exists since the universe must have had a starting point. The divine creator, he believed, is a single, incorporeal being who created the universe out of nothing. Anthropomorphic descriptions of God in the Bible, he argued, should therefore be understood figuratively rather than literally.

---

*Above Statue of Maimonides, the greatest medieval Jewish philosopher, in his birthplace, Cordoba in Spain.*

*Lord*, he wrestled with the question of divine omniscience. In his opinion, God only knows human events if they are determined by heavenly bodies; he does not know them in so far as they are dependent on individual choice. This limitation to divine knowledge, Gersonides believed, is entirely consonant with Scripture and is coherent with the concept of the freedom of the will.

Gersonides was followed by other Jewish philosophers such as the 14th-century Spanish thinker Hasdai Crescas (1340–1410), whose work *The Light of the Lord* offered an alternative account of the basic principles of the Jewish faith in opposition to Maimonides' 13 principles.

However, after Crescas the philosophical approach to religion lost its appeal for most thinkers in Spain. By the end of the 15th century, the impulse to rationalize the Jewish tradition in the light of Greek philosophy had come to an end, and succeeding generations of Jews turned to the mystical tradition as a basis for speculation about God's nature and his creation.

# LURIANIC KABBALAH

IN THE 1500S ISAAC LURIA MADE MAJOR CONTRIBUTIONS TO JEWISH MYSTICISM. HIS INFLUENCE ON A CIRCLE OF DISCIPLES HAD HUGE CONSEQUENCES FOR THE DEVELOPMENT OF KABBALISTIC JUDAISM.

By the early modern period the centre of Kabbalistic activity had shifted to Israel. In this milieu Isaac Luria (1534–72), the greatest mystic of the period, reinterpreted Kabbalistic doctrine – his teaching propounded theories about divine contraction, the shattering of the vessels and cosmic repair. These reflections profoundly influenced the subsequent development of Jewish mysticism.

### MOSES CORDOVERO
One of the greatest mystics of the town of Safed, Moses Cordovero (1522–70), collected, organized and interpreted the teachings of earlier mystical scholars. His work is a systematic summary of the Kabbalah up to his time, and in his most important treatise, *Pardes*, he outlined

*Below A view of Safed and Mount Meron, Israel. Simeon ben Yohai is buried on Mount Meron, and thousands camp out near the tomb on the anniversary of his death on Lag B'Omer, or the 'Scholars' Feast'.*

the Zoharic concepts of the Godhead, the sefirot, the celestial powers and the earthly processes.

In this study he described the sefirot as vessels in which the light of the En Sof is contained and through which it is reflected in different forms. For Cordovero, the Godhead is in this way manifest in every part of the finite world. In another important work, *The Palm Tree of Deborah*, he expressed the notion that in order to achieve the highest degree of the religious life, one should not only observe the commandments but also imitate divine processes and patterns.

### ISAAC LURIA AND CREATION
Originally brought up in Egypt where he studied the Talmud and engaged in business, Isaac Luria withdrew to an island on the Nile where he meditated on the Zohar for seven years. In 1569 he arrived in Safed and died some two years later after having passed on his teaching to a small group of disciples. Of primary

*Above Torah shrine at Ha'ari synagogue in Safed, Israel, where Rabbi Isaac Luria lived and taught.*

importance in the Lurianic system is the mystery of creation. In the literature of early Kabbalists creation was understood as a positive act. For Luria, however, creation was a negative event: the En Sof had to bring into being an empty space in which creation could occur since divine light was everywhere, leaving no room for creation to take place. This was accomplished by the process of *zimzum*, or 'the contraction of the Godhead into itself'.

After this act of withdrawal, a line of light flowed from the Godhead into *tehiru*, or 'empty space', and took on the shape of the sefirot in the form of Adam Kadmon. In this process divine lights created the vessels – the external shapes of the sefirot – which gave specific characteristics to each divine emanation. Yet these vessels were not strong enough to contain such pure light and they shattered. This *shevirat ha-kelim*, or 'breaking of the vessels', brought disaster and upheaval to the emerging emanations: the lower vessels broke down and fell; the three highest emanations were damaged; and the empty space was divided into two parts. The first

part consisted of the broken vessels with many divine sparks clinging to them; the second part was the upper realm where the pure light of God escaped to preserve its purity.

## THE COSMOS

Following the shattering of the vessels the cosmos was divided into two parts: the kingdom of evil in the lower part and the realm of divine light in the upper part. For Luria evil was seen as opposed to existence; therefore it was not able to exist by its own power. Instead it had to derive spiritual force from the divine light. This was accomplished by keeping captive the sparks of the divine light that fell with them when the vessels were broken and subsequently gave sustenance to the satanic domain. Divine attempts to bring unity to all existence now had to focus on the struggle to overcome the evil forces. This was achieved by a continuing process of divine emanation, which at first created the sefirot, the sky, the earth, the Garden of Eden and human beings.

*Below A Hasidic Jew studying in Safed, Israel. The blue colour on the door is thought to protect against the evil eye. Hasidic Judaism is deeply influenced by Kabbalistic thought.*

Humanity was intended to serve as the battleground for this conflict between good and evil. In this regard Adam reflected symbolically the dualism in the cosmos – he possessed a sacred soul while his body represented the evil forces. God's intention was that Adam defeat the evil within himself and bring about Satan's downfall. But when Adam failed, a catastrophe occurred parallel to the breaking of the vessels; instead of divine sparks being saved and uplifted, many new divine lights fell and evil became stronger.

## THE JEWISH PEOPLE

Rather than relying on the action of one person, God then chose the people of Israel to vanquish evil and raise up the captive sparks. The Torah was given to symbolize the Jews' acceptance of this allotted task. When the ancient Israelites undertook to keep the law, redemption seemed imminent. Yet the people of Israel then created the golden calf, a sin parallel to Adam's disobedience. Again, divine sparks fell and the forces of evil were renewed. For Luria, history is a record of attempts by the powers of good to rescue these sparks and unite the divine and earthly spheres. Luria and his disciples believed that they were living

*Above Strictly Orthodox Jews pray for peace in the Lebanon at the grave of mystic Isaac Luria in Safed, Israel.*

in the final stages of this last attempt to overcome evil, in which the coming of the Messiah would signify the end of the struggle.

## TIKKUN

Related to the contraction of God, the breaking of the vessels and the exiled sparks, was Luria's conception of tikkun. This concept refers to the mending of what was broken during the breaking of the vessels. After the catastrophe in the divine realm, the process of restoration began and every disaster was seen as a setback in this process. In this battle, keeping God's commandments was understood as contributing to repair – the divine sparks which fell down can be redeemed by ethical and religious deeds. According to Luria, a spark is attached to all prayers and moral acts; if the Jew keeps the ethical and religious law these sparks are redeemed and lifted up.

By the beginning of the 17th century Lurianic mysticism had had a major impact on Sephardic Jewry, and in succeeding centuries Luria's mystical theology became a central feature of Jewish life.

# KARAITES

THE EMERGENCE OF THE KARAITE MOVEMENT IN THE 8TH CENTURY CE POSED A MAJOR CHALLENGE TO THE RABBINIC ESTABLISHMENT. IT CONTINUED TO EXERT A PROFOUND INFLUENCE ON JEWISH LIFE.

In the early medieval period the emergence of Karaism as an anti-rabbinic movement constituted a major threat to the tradition. Deriving its name from the Hebrew word *mikrah*, or 'Scripture', the Karaites believed that God had revealed his word exclusively in the Written Torah. In their view, the oral Torah as passed down by rabbinic sages was a human reflection on the divine commandments.

### ORIGIN OF THE KARAITES

During the 8th century CE messianic movements appeared in the Persian Jewish community, leading to armed

*Right An 18th-century silver* yad *or finger pointer used when reading from the Torah. For the Karaites the Torah was of pre-eminent importance.*

uprisings against Muslim authorities. Such revolts were quickly crushed, but an even more serious threat to traditional Jewish life was posed later in the century by the emergence of an anti-rabbinic sect, the Karaites. This movement was founded in Babylonia in the 760s by Anan ben David, who had earlier been passed over as exilarch (head of the Jewish community in Babylonia). The Karaites traced its origin to the time

of King Jeroboam in the 8th century BCE. According to some scholars, Anan's movement absorbed elements of an extra-talmudic tradition and took over doctrines from Islam.

The guiding interpretative principle formulated by Anan, 'Search thoroughly in Scripture and do not rely on my opinion', was intended to point to the Bible as the sole source of law. Jewish observances, the Karaites insisted, must conform to biblical legislation rather than rabbinic ordinances. Anan, however, was not lenient concerning legal matters. For example, he did not recognize the minimum quantities of forbidden foods fixed by the rabbis; in addition, he introduced more complicated regulations for circumcision, added to the number of fast days, interpreted the prohibition of work on the Sabbath in stricter terms than the rabbis, and extended the prohibited degrees of marriage. In short, he made the yoke of the law more burdensome.

### THE DEVELOPMENT OF THE KARAITE MOVEMENT

After the death of the founder, new parties within the Karaite movement soon emerged. The adherents of

*Left A prophet of God denounces the idolatry of Jeroboam. Painting by William Hole (1846–1917). For the Karaites God's world was revealed exclusively in Scripture.*

*Above* The Karaite synagogue is the oldest active synagogue in Jerusalem, founded in the 8th century CE. The synagogue is currently below street level, which has risen over the years.

Anan were referred to as the 'Ananites' and remained few in number. In the first half of the 9th century CE, the Ukarite sect was established by Ishmael of Ukbara (near Baghdad). Some years later another sect was formed in the same town by Mishawayh Al-Ukbari. Another group was formed by a contemporary of Mishawayh, Abu Imram Al-Tiflisi. In Israel, yet another sect was established by Malik Al-Ramli. By the end of the 9th century CE, Karaism had become a conglomerate of groups advocating different anti-rabbinic positions, but these sects were short-lived and in time the Karaites consolidated into a uniform movement.

The central representative of mainstream Karaism was Benjamin ben Moses Nahavendi (of Nahavendi in Persia), who advocated a policy of free and independent study of Scripture, which became the dominant ideology of later Karaism. By the 10th century CE, a number

*Right* The Karaite synagogue in Yevpatoria, Ukraine. Yevpatoria became a residence of the Hakham, spiritual leader of the Karaites, when Russia annexed the Crimea in 1738.

of Karaite communities were established in Israel, Iraq and Persia. These groups rejected rabbinic law and devised their own legislation, which led eventually to the foundation of a Karaite rabbinical academy in Jerusalem. There the Karaite community produced some of the most distinguished scholars of the period, who composed legal handbooks, wrote biblical commentaries, expounded on Hebrew philology and engaged in philosophical and theological reflection.

## ANTI-KARAITES AND THE DEVELOPMENT OF KARAISM

The growth of Karaism provoked the rabbis to attack it as a heretical movement. The first prominent authority to engage in anti-Karaite debate was Saadia Gaon, who in the first half of the 9th century CE wrote a book attacking Anan. This polemic was followed by other anti-Karaite tracts by eminent rabbinic authorities.

By the 10th century CE, the Karaites had successfully established a network of synagogues in the Middle East. In addition, the movement produced some of the most distinguished literary figures of eastern Jewry. Karaite scholars composed handbooks of law, wrote commentaries on the Bible, contributed to theology and philosophy, and furthered the growth of Hebrew philology.

However, traditionalists continued to compose diatribes against what they perceived as a heretical sect. But as the social composition of the movement changed, Karaism became less severe, and members of the movement in Egypt and elsewhere became prosperous merchants. As a consequence, the ascetic features of Karaite ritual were modified, and the concept of a post-biblical tradition was gradually accepted.

After the Jerusalem community was destroyed during the First Crusade, the centre of Karaite literary activity shifted to the Byzantine empire. From there Karaites established communities in the Crimea and medieval Poland and Lithuania. In Egypt the Karaite community continued to maintain itself. Subsequently, relations between Karaites and Rabbanites (the rabbinical establishment) varied – at times ties were close whereas at other periods the differences between the Karaism and traditional Judaism were emphasized. Yet, after the 11th century Karaism lost its base of support, and it survived only as a small minority group.

# SHABBATEANS

THE ARRIVAL OF SHABBETAI TZVI ELECTRIFIED THE JEWISH WORLD.
CONVINCED THAT THE LONG-AWAITED MESSIAH HAD COME, FOLLOWERS
ANTICIPATED THAT MESSIANIC REDEMPTION WAS IMMINENT.

Through the centuries, Jews antici-pated the coming of a messianic redeemer who would bring about the transformation of human history. In the middle of the 17th century, Jewry was electrified by the arrival of Shabbetai Tzvi who was pro-claimed the long-awaited Messiah by his disciple Nathan of Gaza. Despite his subsequent apostasy and death in 1676, a circle of followers – the Shabbateans – continued to proclaim his messiahship.

## THE ARRIVAL OF SHABBETAI TZVI

By the beginning of the 17th cen-tury, Lurianic mysticism had made a major impact on Sephardic Jewry, and messianic expectations had also become a central feature of Jewish life. In this milieu the arrival of a self-proclaimed messianic king, Shabbetai Tzvi, brought about a transformation of Jewish life and

*Below A view of 19th-century Smyrna, Turkey, where the false Messiah Shabbetai Tzvi was born in 1626.*

thought. Born in Smyrna into a wealthy family, Shabbetai had received a traditional Jewish educa-tion and later engaged in the study of the Zohar.

After leaving Smyrna in the 1650s Shabbetai spent ten years in various cities in Greece as well as in Constantinople (Istanbul) and Jerusalem. Eventually he became part of a Kabbalistic group in Cairo and travelled to Gaza where he encoun-tered Nathan of Gaza who believed that Shabbetai was the Messiah. In 1665 Shabbetai's messiahship was announced, and Nathan sent letters to Jews in numerous communities asking them to repent and recognize Shabbetai Tzvi as their redeemer. Shabbetai, he announced, would take the Sultan's crown, bring back the lost tribes and inaugurate the period of messianic redemption.

After a brief sojourn in Jerusalem, Shabbetai went to Smyrna, where he encountered strong opposition on the part of some local rabbis. In response he denounced the disbe-lievers and declared that he was the

*Above Shabbetai Tzvi, who declared he was the Messiah or the Anointed of the God of Jacob, engraved in 1666.*

Anointed of the God of Jacob. This action evoked a hysterical response – a number of Jews fell into trances and had visions of him on a royal throne crowned as king of Israel. He journeyed to Constantinople in 1666, but on the order of the grand vizier he was arrested and put into prison. Within a short time the prison quar-ters became a messianic court; pilgrims from all over the world made their way to Constantinople to join in messianic rituals and asce-tic activities. In addition, hymns were written in his honour and new fes-tivals were introduced. According to Nathan who remained in Gaza, the alteration in Shabbetai's moods from illumination to withdrawal symbol-ized his soul's struggle with demonic powers. At times he was imprisoned by the *kelippot*, or 'powers of evil', but at other moments he prevailed against them.

## DEFENDING SHABBETAI'S MESSIAHSHIP

Such an act of apostasy scandalized most of Shabbetai's followers, but he defended himself by asserting he had become a Muslim in obeisance to

God's commands. Many of his followers accepted this explanation and refused to give up their belief. Some thought it was not Shabbetai who had become a Muslim, but rather a phantom who had taken on his appearance; the Messiah himself had ascended to heaven.

Others cited biblical and rabbinic sources to justify Shabbetai's action. Nathan explained that the messianic task involved taking on the humiliation of being portrayed as a traitor to his people.

Furthermore, Nathan argued on the basis of Lurianic Kabbalah that there were two kinds of divine light – a creative light and another light opposed to the existence of anything other than the En Sof (Infinite). While creative light formed structures of creation in empty space, the other light became after *zimzum*, or 'divine contraction', the power of evil. According to Nathan, the soul of the Messiah had been struggling against the power of evil from the beginning; his purpose was to allow divine light to penetrate this domain and bring about *tikkun*, or 'cosmic repair'. In order to do this, the soul of the Messiah was

*Below Interior of the house of Shabbetai Tzvi in Izmir, formerly Smyrna, in Turkey.*

not obligated to keep the law, but was free to descend into the abyss to liberate sparks and thereby conquer evil. In this light, Shabbetai's conversion to Islam was explicable.

## THE SHABBATEAN MOVEMENT

After Shabbetai's act of apostasy, Nathan visited him in the Balkans and then travelled to Rome where he performed secret rites to bring about the end of the Papacy. Shabbetai remained in Adrianople and Constantinople where he lived as both Muslim and Jew. In 1672 he was deported to Albania where he disclosed his own Kabbalistic teaching to his supporters. After he died in 1676, Nathan declared that Shabbetai had ascended to the supernal world.

Eventually a number of groups continued in their belief that Shabbetai Tzvi was the Messiah,

*Above The anointing of Shabbetai Tzvi as King of the Jews by Nathan of Gaza, in a 17th-century engraving.*

including a sect, the Doenmeh, or 'dissidents', which professed Islam publicly but nevertheless adhered to its own traditions. Marrying among themselves, they eventually evolved into antinomian sub-groups, which violated Jewish sexual laws and asserted the divinity of Shabbetai and their leader, Baruchiah Russo.

In Italy several Shabbatean groups also emerged and propagated their views. In the 18th century the most important Shabbatean sect was led by Jacob Frank, who was influenced by the Doenmeh in Turkey. Believing himself to be the incarnation of Shabbetai, Frank announced that he was the second person of the Trinity and gathered together a circle of disciples who indulged in licentious orgies.

# FRANKISTS

IN THE 18TH CENTURY, JACOB FRANK ESTABLISHED A SHABBATEAN
MOVEMENT. ALARMED BY THE RADICAL NATURE OF THIS GROUP, THE
RABBINIC ESTABLISHMENT DENOUNCED THE FRANKISTS AS HERETICS.

The 18th-century Jacob Frank
(1726–91) established a new
Shabbatean group, the Frankists,
whose theology constituted a radical departure from the tradition. Not
surprisingly, Frank and his followers
were anathematized by the rabbinic
establishment for their heretical
views and practices.

## ORIGIN OF THE FRANKISTS

Jacob Frank was born Jacob ben
Judah Leib in Korolowka, a small
town in Podolia. Educated in
Czernowitz and Sniatyn, he lived for
a number of years in Bucharest.
Although he went to heder, or 'Jewish
primary school', he had no knowl-

*Below Caricature of Archbishop
Dembowski of Lemberg, who arranged
a public burning of the Talmud and
other Hebrew writings after the
Shabbateans informed him they
rejected the Talmud in the late 1750s.*

edge of the Talmud. In Bucharest he
began to earn his living as a dealer
in cloth and precious stones.

Frank appears to have been associated with Shabbateans during his
youth. He began to study the Zohar,
making a name in Shabbatean circles as a person possessed of certain
powers. In 1752 he married
Hannah, the daughter of a respected
merchant in Nikopol. Accompanied
by Shabbateans, he visited Salonika
in 1753 and became involved with
the Doenmeh, a radical wing of this
group. Eventually he became the
leader of the Shabbateans in Poland
where he was perceived by his followers as a reincarnation of the
divine soul which had previously
resided in Shabbetai.

Subsequently, Frank journeyed
through the communities of Podolia,
which contained Shabbatean groups.
Although he was received enthusiastically by Shabbateans, Frank's

*Above Jonathan Eybeschutz, rabbi of
the 'Three Communities', was accused
by Jacob Emden of being a secret
Shabbatean. He was cleared in 1753.*

appearance in Lanskroun caused
considerable consternation when he
was discovered conducting a
Shabbatean ritual with his followers
– his Jewish opponents claimed that
a religious orgy was taking place.
Although Frank's followers were
imprisoned, he was released because
the authorities thought he was a
Turkish subject.

At the request of the local rabbis
an enquiry was instituted that examined the practices of the Shabbateans.

## FRANKIST THEOLOGY

In his teaching, Frank revealed himself as the embodiment of God's
power who had come to complete
Shabbetai's task. He was, he believed,
the true Jacob, like Jacob in the Bible
who had completed the work of his
predecessors, Abraham and Isaac. In
short statements and parables, Frank
explained the nature of his mission. It
was necessary, he argued, for those
who belonged to his group to adopt
Christianity outwardly in order to
keep their true faith secret. In his view,
all religions were only stages through
which believers had to pass, like a
person putting on different suits of
clothes that could later be discarded.

*Above Kamenietz: the capital of Podolia in Russian Poland, where the Frankist movement developed.*

In place of the Shabbatean trinity in which all were united in divinity, Frank argued that the true and good God is hidden and divested of any connection with the created order. It is he who conceals himself behind 'the King of Kings'

## THE NEW ROAD

According to Frank all great religious leaders from the patriarchs to Shabbetai Tzvi and Baruchiah, had endeavoured to find the way to God, but failed. In Frank's view, it is necessary to embark on a completely new road, untrodden by the people of Israel. This path is the road to consistent religious anarchy – in order to achieve this goal it is necessary to abolish and destroy Jewish laws, teachings and practices that constrict the power of life. Some believers had already passed through Judaism and Islam; now they had to complete their journey by taking on the Christian faith, using its beliefs and practices to conceal the real core of their belief in Frank as the true Messiah and the living God.

whom Frank also refers to as 'the Great Brother', or 'He who stands before God'. He is the God of the true faith whom one must attempt to approach; in doing so, it is possible to break the domination of the three 'leaders of the world' who rule earth, imposing on it an inappropriate system of law.

## FRANKISTS AND THE CHURCH

Frank prepared his followers to accept baptism as the step that would open before them this new way. Paralleling the pattern in the Gospels, he appointed 12 emissaries who were destined to become his chief disciples. At the same time he appointed 12 'sisters' who were to act as his concubines. Continuing the tradition of the Baruchiah sect, Frank also instituted licentious sexual practices.

As time passed, it became clear that Frank and his followers would need to be baptized, and they requested that Archbishop Lubienski in Lvov receive them into the Church. In making this application, they expressed the desire to be allowed to lead a separate existence. The Church, however, replied that no special privileges would be granted.

In July 1759 a disputation took place in Lvov, as a precondition of conversion, when the leading rabbis and members of the Frankist sect debated a variety of theological topics. In September 1759 Frank was baptized, and by the end of 1760 in Lvov alone more than 500 Frankists followed his example. Despite such widespread conversion, the Church became increasingly suspicious of the Frankists: it appeared that the real object of their devotion was Frank as the living incarnation of God.

In February 1760 Frank was arrested and an inquisition took place, resulting in Frank's imprisonment, though he was later released. In 1791 Frank died, mourned by hundreds of his followers.

*Below Street in the Jewish area of Lvov, in the Ukraine, where a Frankist disputation took place in 1759.*

CHAPTER 3

# MODERN JUDAISM

On the far right of the religious spectrum, Orthodox Judaism and Hasidism hold tenaciously to the belief system of the past, believing the Torah in its entirety was given by God to Moses on Mount Sinai; in addition, the rabbinic interpretation of the law is sacrosanct. However, recent times have seen the emergence of new forms of Judaism with radically different ideologies some of which do not accept the Torah as the basis of Jewish life.

In the early 19th century, Reform Jews were anxious to modernize the tradition. They felt it was no longer necessary for Jews to adhere to the minutiae of the law and set aside certain central tenets of traditional Judaism. Conservative Jews adopted a less radical view, yet also sought to make Judaism relevant in the modern world. More recently, Reconstructionist and Humanistic Jews argued that Judaism must divest itself from supernaturalism. A growing number of Jews sought to revitalize the faith through Jewish renewal. And, at the margin of Jewish life, Messianic Jews believed that a new era had dawned with the coming of the messianic age.

*Opposite A Hasidic Jew, arms outstretched with joy, celebrates the reunification of Jerusalem on the first Jerusalem Day in 1968. He is carried by a soldier at the Western Wall.*

**Above** *In 1954, US architect Frank Lloyd Wright designed his only synagogue, Beth Shalom at Elkins Park, Pennsylvania, a startling modernist version of an ancient temple.*

# ORTHODOX JUDAISM

BOUND BY THE JEWISH LEGAL SYSTEM, ORTHODOX JEWS KEEP ALIVE THE TRADITIONS OF THEIR ANCESTORS. THE RITUALS OF ORTHODOX JUDAISM BRING THE CHAIN OF TRADITION INTO THE PRESENT AGE.

The origins of Orthodox Judaism stretch back 4,000 years to the birth of the Jewish nation. From the time of the patriarchs to rabbinic Judaism, Jews were bound by the covenant with Moses. Orthodox Jews today adhere to the tenets of the faith in an uncompromising fashion.

## ORIGINS OF ORTHODOXY

Orthodox Judaism is the branch of Judaism that adheres most strictly to halakha, or 'Jewish law'. By the 18th century local Jewish communities had lost much of their authority. This led to the disintegration of the traditional religious establishment as well as the prestige of communal leaders. Coupled with the aspirations of Jewish emancipationists, new interpretations of the faith and an altered conception of the relationship between Jews and non-Jews, Orthodox Judaism was a response to these changes in Jewish life.

*Below Sephardic Mordechai Eliyahu and Ashkenazi Avraham Shapira were Orthodox chief rabbis of Israel, 1983–93.*

In the first half of the 19th century, traditionalist Jews in Hungary and Germany were profoundly critical of the efforts of Reform Jews to adapt halakha to modern society as well as modify the traditional synagogue service. These reformers argued such alterations were a condition for Jewish emancipation as well as civil equality. Traditionalists viewed this attitude a violation of God's will.

At the end of the 19th century, Eastern European Orthodox leaders similarly championed Torah Judaism in the face of increased secularism.

## ORTHODOX THEOLOGY

Until the growth of the Enlightenment in the 18th century, the Jewish people affirmed their belief in one God who created the universe. As a transcendent deity he brought all things into being, continues to sustain the cosmos, and guides humanity to its ultimate destiny. In the unfolding of this providential scheme, Israel has a central role – as God's chosen people, the nation is to serve as a light to all peoples.

*Above A strictly Orthodox family in Jerusalem. Note the girls' sober clothing and the boy's side curls and fringes.*

Scripture does not contain a dogmatic formulation of such beliefs, but the Orthodox prayer book contains the medieval philosopher Moses Maimonides' formulation of the '13 Principles of the Jewish Faith'.

As Maimonides explained, anyone who denies any of these tenets is to be regarded as a heretic: God's existence; God's unity; God's incorporeality; God's eternity; God alone is to be worshipped; prophecy; Moses is the greatest of the prophets; the divine origin of the Torah (Pentateuch); the Torah is immutable; God knows the thoughts and deeds of human beings; reward and punishment; the Messiah; resurrection of the dead. Maimonides' principles as well as parallel dogmatic formulations by other medieval thinkers served as the basis for theological speculation through the centuries.

## MODERN TRADITIONALISTS

Today Orthodox Jews continue to subscribe to these fundamental doctrines, secure in the knowledge that they are fulfilling God's will. Such a commitment serves as the framework for the traditional Orthodox way of life. Wary of modernity, traditional Orthodox Jews are anxious to preserve the Jewish way of life through a process of intensive

*Right Friday night in Jerusalem. Jewish tradition encourages everyone to dress finely for Shabbat.*

education – for these Jews there can be no compromise with secularism. Such attitudes permeate all aspects of Jewish life from the earliest age. Among traditional Orthodox Jews, education for boys is rigorous, following the curriculum laid down in ancient times. Within strictly Orthodox circles, expectations for girls are of a different nature; Jewish young women are reared to become loyal and dedicated mothers and homemakers.

Strict adherence to Jewish law is demanded within the context of traditional orthodoxy. Committed to the doctrine of Torah Mi Sinai (the belief that God revealed the Torah to Moses on Mount Sinai), Orthodox Jews are obliged to keep all biblical and rabbinic ordinances. To accomplish this in a modern setting requires both determination and scrupulous care. Although the traditional Orthodox constitute only a minority of the Jewish community, there is a growing element anxious to draw other Jews to the traditional faith.

*Below Pupils crowd round the desk of a teacher at an Orthodox elementary school in Jerusalem.*

## ORTHODOX JUDAISM TODAY

The dominant trend in Orthodoxy since World War II has been its increased emphasis of adherence to the traditional Jewish way of life. What is required is religious zealotry, observance of the mitzvot, or commandments, and a rejection of modern values and culture.

Throughout the Jewish world, Orthodox Jews have actively encouraged the establishment of schools, synagogues, political organizations, a press and summer camps. Both Orthodox rabbis and lay leaders have been anxious to counter the threats of secularism and modernity.

Today most Orthodox Jews reside in Israel or the United States. In Israel religiously observant Jews make up about 15–20 per cent of the Jewish population. These neo-traditionalists, who were once marginal to Israeli society, play an increasingly important role in communal and political life. Within their ranks the Edah Haredit (community of the pious) consist of thousands of families with numerous sympathizers. These are the most intransigent of the Orthodox. They relate to the state of Israel with various degrees of hostility. A more moderate neotraditionalism is found in Israeli Agudah circles.

Among Israeli Orthodox Jews, the heads of the yeshivot and a number of Hasidic rebbes are dominant. In the United States, neo-traditionalists have been supportive of their own institutions.

With the exception of pockets of neo-traditional extremists such as the Edah Haredit in Israel, American Orthodox Jews are generally familiar with modern culture, and most are willing to work with the non-Orthodox on behalf of general Jewish interests.

*Below An Orthodox Jew wearing the traditional prayer shawl and tefillin, boxes worn on the forehead and arm.*

# HASIDISM

SINCE THE 18TH CENTURY HASIDISM HAS BEEN A POWERFUL FORCE IN JEWISH LIFE. TODAY THE HASIDIC COMMUNITY IS DIVIDED INTO A NUMBER OF SUB-GROUPS, EACH WITH ITS OWN REBBE.

In the 18th century, Hasidism emerged as a challenge to the rabbinic establishment. Founded by the Ba'al Shem Tov (1700–60), the movement stressed the importance of eliminating selfhood and the ascent of the soul to divine light. Unlike the arid scholasticism of traditional Judaism, Hasidism offered to the Jewish masses a new outlet for religious fervour.

## THE ORIGINS OF HASIDISM

During the second half of the 18th century, this new popular movement attracted thousands of followers. Pietistic in orientation, Hasidism was based on Kabbalistic ideas and reinterpreted the role of the rabbi as a spiritual guide. It first appeared in the villages of the Polish Ukraine, especially Podolia, where Shabbatean Frankists had been active. According

*Below A Hasidic Jew holds the lulav and etrog in a sukkah built for Sukkot in Williamsburg, New York.*

to tradition, Israel ben Eliezer, known as the Ba'al Shem Tov or Besht, was born in Southern Poland and in his twenties journeyed with his wife to the Carpathian mountains. In the 1730s he travelled to Mezhbizh where he performed various miracles and instructed his disciples in Kabbalistic lore. By the 1740s he had attracted a considerable number of disciples who passed on his teaching. After his death in 1760, Dov Baer became the leader of this sect and Hasidism spread to southern Poland, the Ukraine and Lithuania.

## CRITICISM

The growth of Hasidism engendered considerable hostility on the part of rabbinic authorities. In particular the rabbinic leadership of Vilna issued an edict of excommunication. The Hasidim were charged with permissiveness in their observance of the commandments, laxity in the study of the Torah, excess in prayer, and preference for

*Above Hasidic women behind a mechitza screen that affords them a limited view of the service at Viznitz synagogue, Stamford Hill, London.*

the Lurianic rather than the Ashkenazic prayer book. In subsequent years the Hasidim and their opponents (Mitnaggedim) bitterly denounced one another. Relations deteriorated further when Jacob Joseph of Polonnoye published a book critical of the rabbinate; his work was burned, and in 1791 the Mitnaggedim ordered that all relations with the Hasidim cease.

By the end of the century, the Jewish religious establishment of Vilna denounced the Hasidim to the Russian government, an act resulting in the imprisonment of several leaders. Despite such condemnation, the movement was eventually recognized by the Russian and Austrian governments. In the ensuing years the movement divided into a number of separate groups under different leaders who passed on positions of authority to their descendants.

## HASIDIC THEOLOGY

Hasidism initiated a profound change in Jewish religious pietism. In the medieval period, the Hasidei Ashkenaz attempted to achieve perfection through various mystical activities. This tradition was carried on by Lurianic Kabbalists who engaged in various forms of self-

***Above*** *Dancing at a Chabad-Lubavitch bar mitzvah in Paris in 2008. Chabad-Lubavitch is now one of the largest Hasidic organizations in the world.*

mortification. In opposition to such ascetic practices, the Ba'al Shem Tov and his followers emphasized the omnipresence of God rather than the shattering of the vessels and the imprisonment of divine sparks by the powers of evil. For Hasidic Judaism there is no place where God is absent; the doctrine of *zimzum*, or 'divine contraction', was interpreted by Hasidic sages as only an apparent withdrawal of the divine light. Divine light, they believed, is everywhere. As the Ba'al Shem Tov explained, in every one of a person's troubles, physical and spiritual, even in that trouble God himself is there.

For some Hasidim, devekut, or 'cleaving to God in prayer', was understood as the annihilation of selfhood and the ascent of the soul to divine light. In this context joy, humility, gratitude and spontaneity were seen as essential features of Hasidic worship. The central obstacles to concentration in prayer are distracting thoughts; according to Hasidism, such sinful intentions contain a divine spark which can be released. In this regard, the traditional

***Right*** *The Rebbe and his Hasidim during Hanukkah at the Premishlan congregation in Bnei Brak, Israel.*

Kabbalistic stress on theological speculation was replaced by a preoccupation with mystical psychology in which inner bliss was conceived as the highest aim rather than *tikkun*, or 'repair of the cosmos'.

For the Hasidim, it was also possible to achieve devekut in daily activities including eating, drinking, business affairs and sex. Such ordinary acts became religious if in performing them one cleaves to God, and devekut is thus attainable by all Jews rather than just by a scholarly elite. Unlike the earlier mystical tradition, Hasidism provided a means by which ordinary Jews could reach a state of spiritual ecstasy. Hasidic worship embraced singing, dancing and joyful devotion in anticipation of the period of messianic redemption.

### THE ZADDIK

Another central feature of this new movement was the institution of the zaddik, which gave expression to a widespread disillusionment with rabbinic leadership. According to Hasidism, the zaddikim are spiritually superior individuals who have attained the highest level of devekut. The goal of the zaddik was to elevate the souls of his flock to the divine light. His tasks included

***Above*** *Rabbi Menachem Schneerson giving funds to a follower as a blessing. He led the Chabad-Lubavitch movement in the late 20th century.*

pleading to God for his people, immersing himself in their everyday affairs, and counselling and strengthening them. As an authoritarian figure, the zaddik was seen by his followers as possessing the miraculous power to ascend to the divine realm. In this context, devekut to God involved cleaving to the zaddik. Given this emphasis on the role of the zaddik, Hasidic literature included summaries of the spiritual and Kabbalistic teachings of various famous zaddikim as well as stories about their miraculous deeds.

# CONSERVATIVE JUDAISM

CONSERVATIVE JUDAISM ADOPTS A MIDDLE POSITION BETWEEN ORTHODOX AND REFORM JUDAISM, ADVOCATING LOYALTY TO THE TRADITION COUPLED WITH AN ACCEPTANCE OF MODERN VALUES.

In the wake of the Enlightenment of the 18th century, reformers sought to modernize the Jewish tradition. Initially, Reform Judaism constituted a radically new approach to the tradition. Yet more conservative reformers were alarmed by the radicalism of their co-religionists. Eventually, Conservative Judaism emerged as a more moderate form of Jewish modernism.

## ZACHARIAS FRANKEL

The founder of what came to be known as Conservative Judaism was Zacharias Frankel (1801–75). An advocate of moderate reform, Frankel was committed to a historically evolving dynamic Judaism. The aim of such an approach (positive historical Judaism), he believed, would be to uncover the origins of the Jewish people's national spirit and the collective will. Both the past as enshrined in tradition and the present as embodied in the religious consciousness of the people, he argued, should determine the nature of Jewish life.

In 1845 Frankel left the Reform rabbinical conference in Frankfurt because a majority of the participants had voted that there was no need to use Hebrew in the Jewish worship service. Although he agreed with other reformers that Judaism needed to be revised, he disputed with them over the legitimate criteria for religious change. None the less, he broke with Orthodoxy in asserting that the Oral law was rabbinic in origin, that the halakha, or 'Jewish law', had evolved over time, and that the source of religious observance was not divine.

## SOLOMON SCHECHTER

In the United States a similar approach to the tradition was adopted by a number of leading figures including

*Above Seder plate showing traditional foods eaten at Passover – an egg, lamb, green vegetables, haroset and bitter herbs. Conservative Judaism stresses the importance of ritual in Jewish life.*

the Jewish scholar Solomon Schechter (1847–1915) who argued that Conservative Judaism should combine elements of both traditional and non-traditional Judaism. Disdainfully Schechter rejected both Reform and Orthodoxy. Instead, he emphasized the importance of traditional rituals, customs, observances as well as belief, while simultaneously stressing the need for a historical perspective.

In February 1913 a union of 22 congregations was founded, committed to maintaining the Jewish tradition in its historical continuity. In the preamble to its constitution, the United Synagogue stated its intention to separate from Reform Judaism – it was committed to a heterogeneous, traditional mode of belief and practice through the observance of ritual in the home and synagogue. As Conservative Judaism expanded in the 1920s and 1930s a degree of uniformity developed in congregational worship. Services usually began late Friday evening and early Saturday morning; head coverings were required; prayer shawls were usually worn on

*Left Prime Minister David Ben-Gurion of Israel and Louis Finkelstein, Chancellor of the Jewish Seminary for Conservative Judaism, New York, look at rare books at the seminary, 1960.*

Sabbath morning; rabbis conducted the service and preached English sermons; prayer books other than the Union Prayer Book of the Reform movement were used; and many congregants participated in afternoon study with the rabbi. In addition, many synagogues had organs, mixed choirs, family pews, and *minyans*, or 'quorum for a religious service', that met three times a day for prayer.

## CONSERVATIVE THEOLOGY

Conservative Jews viewed Judaism as an evolving organism that remained spiritually vibrant by adjusting to environmental and cultural conditions. In consequence, Conservative thinkers attempted to preserve those elements of the tradition that they believed to be spiritually meaningful while simultaneously setting aside those observances that actually hinder the continued growth of Judaism. Such obsolete practices were not abrogated, but simply ignored. In a similar spirit, Conservative Jews, in contrast with the Orthodoxy, felt no compulsion to accept theological doctrines which they believed were outmoded – thus Conservative Judaism broke with Orthodoxy regarding the belief that the Torah was revealed in its entirety to Moses on Mount Sinai.

In its quest to modernize the faith, Conservative scholars sought to establish an authoritative body to adapt Judaism to contemporary circumstances. As early as 1918 there was a considerable desire to establish a body of men learned in the law who would be able to advise the movement concerning pressing contemporary issues. Thus, even though the Conservative movement refused to formulate a detailed platform or series of credal statements, these features of Conservative Judaism provided a coherent and imaginative approach to the tradition.

*Above In 1963, Martin Luther King received the Solomon Schechter Award. Schechter (1847–1915) was a leading figure of the Conservative movement.*

## CONSERVATIVE BELIEFS

Regarding belief in God, Conservative thinkers have generally subscribed to the traditional understanding of the Deity as omnipotent, omniscient, and all-good. Yet, in contrast with Orthodoxy, there remains considerable ambiguity about the nature of divine communication. Unlike Orthodox thinkers who view revelation as verbal in nature and Reform theologians who conceive of the Torah as a largely human product, the Conservative movement has generally attempted to bridge these two extremes. Within Conservative Judaism revelation is understood as a divinely initiated process involving human composition. As to what constitutes the nature of such a divine human encounter, Conservative writers vary: some argue that human beings correctly recorded the divine will as revealed at Sinai; others that those who wrote the Scriptures were simply divinely inspired.

Regarding halakha, Conservative thinkers emphasized the importance of conserving the laws of traditional Judaism, including dietary observances, Sabbath, festival and liturgical prescriptions, and ethical precepts. Nevertheless, Conservative scholars advocated change and renewal. On the whole they stressed the historical importance of the Jewish heritage. Guided by such an approach to law, the Conservative movement resorted to what Schechter called 'the conscience of catholic Israel' in reaching decisions about the status of biblical and rabbinic law.

Concerning Jewish peoplehood, the Conservative movement has consistently affirmed the pre-eminence of K'lal Yisrael, or 'the body of Israel'. Yet despite this insistence there has not been the same unanimity about the nation of God's chosen people. Although the Sabbath and High Holy Day prayer books have retained the traditional formula ('You have chosen us from all the nations'), there has been a wide diversity of interpretation of the concept of chosenness among Conservative thinkers. Yet, as a consequence of its dedication to the peoplehood of Israel, the Conservative movement has from its inception been dedicated to the founding of the State of Israel.

# REFORM JUDAISM

THE ENLIGHTENMENT HAD A DEEP IMPACT; NO LONGER WERE JEWS FORCED TO LIVE IN GHETTOS. REFORM JUDAISM EMERGED AS A REVOLUTIONARY MOVEMENT WHOSE AIM WAS TO MODERNIZE THE FAITH.

At the end of the 18th century, such advocates of Jewish enlightenment as Moses Mendelssohn encouraged fellow Jews to integrate into the mainstream of western European culture. Subsequently early reformers tried to reform Jewish education by widening the traditional curriculum of Jewish schools. Pre-eminent among these figures was Israel Jacobson, who founded a boarding school for boys in Westphalia and subsequently established other schools throughout the kingdom. In these new foundations, general subjects were taught by Christian teachers while a Jewish instructor gave lessons about Judaism.

Simultaneously a number of Reform temples were opened in Germany with innovations to the liturgy, including prayers and sermons in German as well as choral singing and organ music. The central

*Below The West London Synagogue of British Jews, founded 1840. They chose this name to emphasize their patriotism.*

aim of these early reformers was to adapt Jewish worship to contemporary aesthetic standards. For these innovators, the informality of the traditional service seemed foreign and undignified. They therefore insisted on greater decorum, more unison in prayer, a choir, hymns and music responses, as well as alterations in prayers and service length.

## REFORMING JUDAISM

In response to such developments, Orthodoxy asserted that any change to the tradition was a violation of the Jewish heritage. For these traditionalists the Written and Oral Torah constitute an infallible chain of divinely revealed truth. Despite this reaction, some German rabbis began to re-evalute the Jewish tradition. In this undertaking the achievements of Jewish scholars who engaged in the scientific study of Judaism had a profound impact. In Frankfurt the Society of Friends of Reform was founded and published a proclamation stating that they recognized the

*Above US Reform rabbi Isaac Mayer Wise became President of the Hebrew Union College, the rabbinical seminary of the Reform movement in 1875.*

possibility of unlimited progress in the Jewish faith and rejected the authority of the legal code as well as the belief in messianic redemption.

A similar group was founded in Berlin in 1844 and called for major changes in the Jewish tradition. That year the first Reform synod took place at Brunswick in which the participants formulated a programme of reform. This was followed by a series of synods. In England similar developments took place with the establishment of the West London Synagogue in the 1840s. In the USA, Reform congregations were established first in Charleston, South Carolina and later in New York City. Isaac Mayer Wise founded the Union of American Hebrew Congregations with lay and rabbinical representatives in 1873, and the Hebrew Union College, the first Reform rabbinical seminary in America in 1875.

## PHILOSOPHY

In 1885 a gathering of Reform rabbis met in Pittsburgh, Pennsylvania, and adopted a programme of reform: the Pittsburgh Platform. This document insisted on a number of central principles of this new movement. According to these reformers,

*Above Reform rabbi Sally Priesand
was ordained in 1972. She is reputedly
the world's first woman rabbi.*

Judaism presents the highest conception of the God-idea as taught in holy Scripture and developed and spiritualized by Jewish teachers. They believed the Bible is the record of the consecration of the Jewish people to its divine mission, yet it should be subjected to scientific research. The Mosaic legislation, they declared, is a system of training the Jewish people, but today only the moral laws are binding; rabbinic legislation is apt to obstruct rather than further modern spiritual elevation. Further, the reformers rejected the belief in the Messiah as well as the doctrine of heaven and hell. It is the duty of modern Jewry, they asserted, to strive for justice in modern society.

Fifty years after the Pittsburgh meeting of 1885, the Jewish world had undergone major changes: America had become the centre of the Diaspora; Zionism had become a vital force in Jewish life; and Hitler was in power.

The Columbus Platform of the Reform movement adopted in 1937 reflected a new approach to liberal Judaism. In later years the Reform movement underwent further change. In the 1960s new liturgies were used, and in the 1970s a new Reform prayer book was published

which changed the content as well as the format of worship. In 1972 the first woman rabbi was ordained, and by the early 1980s more than 75 women had entered the rabbinate. In 1976 the Reform movement produced the San Francisco Platform – the purpose of this statement was to provide a unifying document which would bring a sense of order to the movement.

More recently, another platform was issued by the Central Conference of American Rabbis in 1991. At the onset of the 21st century, this rabbinic body set out a new statement of principles that affirmed the central tenets of Judaism – God, Torah and Israel – while acknowledging the diversity of Reform Jewish belief and practice. In this platform the movement affirmed the reality and

oneness of God despite the differing theological interpretations. Further, it affirmed that the Jewish people are bound to God by an eternal covenant and that all human beings are created in the image of God. The Torah was conceived as the foundation of Jewish life; in this context the study of Hebrew, the language of Torah and the Jewish liturgy were extolled. The Jewish quest to bring Torah into the world was regarded as a central aspect of the faith. Finally, the movement stressed that the Reform movement is committed to strengthening the people of Israel and to furthering the interests of the Jewish State.

*Below A Reform Yom Kippur service
held at the Reform Temple De Hirsch
Sinai, Seattle, Washington.*

# RECONSTRUCTIONIST JUDAISM

SEEKING TO MODERNIZE THE CENTRAL TENETS OF THE FAITH, RECONSTRUCTIONIST JUDAISM EMERGED IN THE EARLY 1900s AS A RADICAL ALTERNATIVE TO MAINSTREAM JEWISH MOVEMENTS.

The Reconstructionist movement emerged in the first half of the 20th century in the United States as a radical interpretation of the faith. Inspired by its founder, Mordecai Kaplan (1881–1983), the movement rejected the concept of a supernatural deity, and focused on the sociological dimensions of the tradition. Reconstructionists view Judaism as an evolving religious civilization in which spiritual symbols play a fundamental role.

## ORIGINS

Unlike Reform and Conservative Judaism, Reconstructionist Judaism developed out of the thinking of an individual teacher. Born in Lithuania in 1881, Mordecai Kaplan served as

*Below* The Reconstructionist, *1959. Since 1935 the magazine has traced the growth of Reconstructionist Judaism in North America.*

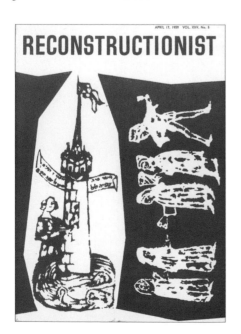

professor of homiletics at the Jewish Theological Seminary in New York. During the 1910s and 1920s he engaged in wide-ranging congregational work; later he officiated as a rabbi at a synagogue-centre in New York. In 1922 Kaplan initiated a policy of reconstructing Judaism to meet the demands of modern life. After publishing *Judaism as a Civilization* in 1934, he launched the *Reconstructionist* magazine.

In *Judaism as a Civilization* Kaplan evaluated the main religious groupings of American society. In his view, Reform had correctly recognized the evolving character of Judaism, yet it ignored the social basis of Jewish identity as well as the organic character of Jewish peoplehood. Neo-Orthodoxy, on the other hand, acknowledged Judaism as a way of life and provided an intensive programme of Jewish education. None the less, it mistakenly regarded the Jewish religion as unchanging. In contrast, Conservative Judaism was committed to the scientific study of the history of the Jewish faith while recognizing the unity of the Jewish people. However it was too closely bound to the halakha, or 'Jewish law' to respond to new circumstances. All of these movements failed to adjust adequately to the modern age; what was needed, Kaplan argued, was a definition of Judaism as an evolving religious civilization.

## A RECONSTRUCTED JUDAISM

In the light of this vision of a reconstructed Judaism, Kaplan called for the re-establishment of a network of organic Jewish communities that

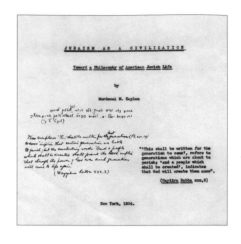

*Above First page of the manuscript of Mordecai Kaplan's* Judaism as a Civilization, *dated New York, 1934, with handwritten notes by Kaplan.*

would ensure the self-perpetuation of the Jewish heritage. Membership of this new movement would be voluntary; leadership should be elected democratically; and private religious opinions would be respected. Kaplan proposed a worldwide Jewish assembly, which would adopt a covenant defining the Jews as a trans-national people. In Kaplan's

*Below Mordecai Kaplan, founder of Reconstructionist Judaism, at Camp Modin, Maine, 1958. Modin began in 1922 as 'The Camp with a Jewish Idea'.*

Many of the ideas found in Kaplan's writings were reflected in the movement's religious literature. *The New Haggadah for Passover*, for example, applied Kaplan's theology to liturgical texts, subordinating miracles and plagues in the traditional Haggadah to the narrative of Israel's redemption from Egypt. *The Sabbath Prayer Book* was designed for those who were dissatisfied with synagogue worship – its aim was to arouse emotion by eliminating theologically untenable passages and adding inspirational material drawn from the tradition. This new prayer book deleted all references to the revelation of the Torah on Mount Sinai, the chosenness of Israel, and the doctrine of a personal Messiah.

*Above Reconstructionist rabbi Sharon Kleinbaum dances the Hora, a popular Jewish circle dance, after officiating at a same-sex wedding in New York, 2010.*

view, religion is the concretization of the collective self-consciousness of the group, which is manifest in spiritual symbols such as persons, places, events and writings. These symbols inspire feelings of reverence, commemorate what the group believes to be most valuable, provide historical continuity, and strengthen the collective consciousness of the people. In order for the Jewish community to survive, Kaplan believed it must eliminate its authoritarian dogmatic features.

## SUPERNATURAL BELIEF
In particular, Judaism must divest itself of supernatural belief. The spiritual dimension of the faith must be reformed in humanistic and naturalistic terms. For Kaplan, God is not a supernatural being but the power that makes for salvation. God, he wrote, is the sum of all the animating organizing forces and relationships that are forever making a cosmos out of chaos. In Kaplan's view, the idea of God must be understood fundamentally in terms of its effect. In his view, God is a 'trans-national', 'super-factual' and 'super-experiential' transcendence, which does not infringe on the laws of nature. Such a notion was far-removed from

the biblical and rabbinic concept of God as the creator and sustainer of the universe who chose the Jewish people and guides humanity to its final destiny.

## THE MOVEMENT
In the 1940s and 1950s the leaders of Reconstructionist Judaism insisted they were not attempting to form a new branch of Judaism. Throughout this period, Reconstructionists hoped to be able to infuse the three major groups within North American Judaism (Orthodox, Conservative and Reform) with its ideas.

However, by the end of the 1960s the Reconstructionist movement had become a denomination – it had established a seminary to train Reconstructionist rabbis and had instituted a congregational structure. Regarding halakha or Jewish law,

the Reconstructionist Rabbinical Association issued a statement of its 1980 convention that placed authority in the Jewish people (as opposed to the rabbis) and created a process whereby each congregation would be free to evolve its own *minhag*, or 'customs'. Three years later, the Association produced guidelines on intermarriage, encouraging rabbis to welcome mixed couples (a Jew and a non-Jew), permit them to participate in Jewish synagogue life, and recognize their children as Jewish if raised as Jews. In addition, the Association decreed that rabbis could sanctify an intermarriage as long as it was accompanied by a civil, rather than a religious, ceremony.

*Below Celebrating Sukkot at the Reconstructionist Rabbinical College in Wyncote, Pennsylvania, USA.*

# HUMANISTIC JUDAISM

THIS RADICAL MOVEMENT HAS BECOME AN ALTERNATIVE FOR SOME JEWS. IT OFFERS JEWISH SECULAR HUMANISTS A NEW FORM OF JUDAISM DEVOID OF A BELIEF IN A SUPERNATURAL DEITY.

Like Reconstructionist Judaism, Jewish humanism offers a non-theistic interpretation of the Jewish faith. Originating in the 1960s in Detroit, Michigan under the leadership of Rabbi Sherwin Wine, Humanistic Judaism now numbers about 40,000 members in the United States, Israel, Europe and elsewhere. The movement originated in 1965, when the Birmingham Temple in a suburb outside Detroit began to publicize its philosophy of Judaism. In 1966 a special committee for Humanistic Judaism was organized at the Temple to share service and educational material with rabbis and laity. The following year a meeting of several leaders of the movement met, issuing a statement, which affirmed that Judaism should be governed by

*Below Blowing the Shofar for Yom Kippur at a humanistic service at Morris County, NJ, USA, 2005.*
*In a break with tradition, the service is about atonement – but not to God.*

empirical reason and human needs. A new magazine, *Humanistic Judaism* was founded. Two years later, two new Humanistic congregations were established: Temple Beth Or in Deerfield, Illinois, and a Congregation for Humanistic Judaism in Fairfield County, Connecticut.

In 1969 the Society for Humanistic Judaism was established in Detroit to provide a basis for cooperation among Humanistic Jews, and in 1970 the first annual conference of the Society took place. During the next ten years new congregations were established in Boston, Toronto, Los Angeles, Washington, Miami, Long Beach and Huntington, New York. In subsequent years Secular Humanistic Judaism became an international movement with supporters on five continents. The National Federation currently comprises nine national organizations in the United States, Canada, Britain, France, Belgium, Israel, Australia, Argentina and Uruguay.

*Above Rabbi Sherwin Wine founded the Society for Humanistic Judaism in North America, in 1969.*

## THE IDEOLOGY OF HUMANISTIC JUDAISM

In 1986 the Federation issued a proclamation stating its ideology and aims. According to this document, Humanistic Jews value human reason and the reality of the world which reason discloses. In their view, the natural universe stands on its own, requiring no supernatural intervention. In this light, Humanists believe in the value of human existence and in the power of human beings to solve their problems individually and collectively. Life, they maintain, should be directed to the satisfaction of human needs. In their view, Judaism, as the civilization of Jews, is a human creation: it embraces all manifestations of Jewish life, including Jewish languages, ethical traditions, historic memories, cultural heritage, and especially the emergence of the state of Israel in modern times.

The Jewish people, Humanists insist, is a world with a pluralistic culture and civilization all its own. Judaism, as the culture of the Jews, is thus more than theological content. It encompasses many languages, a vast body of literature, historical memories and ethical values. Yet, unlike other modern movements, Humanistic Judaism seeks to

welcome all people who seek to identify with Jewish culture and destiny. Hence, Humanists have redefined the notion of Jewishness. A Jew, they state, is a person of Jewish descent or any person who declares himself or herself to be a Jew and who identifies with the history, ethical values, culture, civilization, and community of the Jewish nation.

## JEWISH FESTIVALS

Dedicated to Jewish survival, Humanistic Judaism emphasizes the importance of Jewish festivals in fostering Jewish identity. Yet, for Humanistic Jews, they must be detached from their supernatural origins and reinterpreted in the light of modern circumstances. Such a reorientation provides a basis for extolling human potential.

So, too, does Humanistic Judaism's understanding of life-cycle events: the ceremonies connected with these events emphasize the importance of group survival. Beginning with birth, Humanistic Jews stress the connection of the child with the future of the family, the Jewish people and humanity. Likewise, Humanistic Judaism fosters a Humanistic maturity ceremony, which reflects the ethical commitments of Humanistic

Jews. As an important transitional event, the marriage ceremony should also embody Humanistic values. For Humanistic Jews, the wedding should embrace the conception of the bride and groom publicly declaring their commitment and support and loyalty to one another.

Rituals connected with death should similarly be expressive of Humanistic principles. Humanistic Judaism asserts that mortality is an unavoidable and final event. Accepting this truth, it is possible to live courageously and generously in the face of tragedy. A Humanistic Jewish memorial service serves as

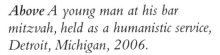

*Above A young man at his bar mitzvah, held as a humanistic service, Detroit, Michigan, 2006.*

an opportunity to teach a philosophy of life. Both the meditations and the eulogies are designed to remind people that the value of personal life lies in its quality, not in its quantity.

## A NEW APPROACH

Humanistic Judaism, then, offers an option for those who wish to identify with the Jewish community despite their rejection of the traditional understanding of God's nature and activity. Unlike Reconstructionist Judaism, with its emphasis on the observances of the past, Humanistic Judaism fosters a radically new approach. The Jewish heritage is relevant only in so far as it advances Humanistic ideals.

In addition, traditional definitions and principles are set aside in the quest to create a Judaism consonant with a scientific and pluralistic age. Secular in orientation, Humanistic Jews seek to create a world in which the Jewish people are dedicated to the betterment of all humankind.

*Left Altar at a humanistic wedding scattered with natural objects – flowers, stones, incense and a glass goblet.*

# JEWISH RENEWAL

FOSTERING A NON–TRADITIONAL COMMITMENT TO JEWISH HERITAGE, JEWISH RENEWAL IS A PRODUCT OF THE COUNTER–CULTURE MOVEMENTS, ORGANIZED AROUND EXPERIMENTAL FELLOWSHIPS.

The Jewish Renewal movement brings Kabbalistic and Hasidic theory and practice into a non-Orthodox, egalitarian framework. In this respect, Jewish Renewal is characterized by its Hasidic orientation. Renewal Jews often add ecstatic practices such as meditation, chant and dance to traditional worship. In addition, some Renewal Jews borrow from Buddhism, Sufism and other faiths to enhance their spiritual approach.

## HISTORY

Jewish renewal has its origins in the North American counter-movements of the late 1960s and early 1970s. During this period, a number of young rabbis, academics and political activists founded experimental havurot, or 'fellowships', for prayer and study in a reaction to what they perceived as the overly organized institutional structures of mainstream Judaism. Initially the main inspiration was the pietistic fellowship of the Pharisees as well as other early

sects. In addition, some of these groups attempted to function as fully fledged communes after the model of their secular counterparts. Others formed communities within urban and suburban contexts.

Founders of the havurot movement included the liberal political activist Arthur Waskow, Conservative rabbi Michael Strassfeld and perhaps Jewish Renewal's most prominent leader, Zalman Schachter-Shalomi. Even though the original leadership consisted of men, US Jewish feminists were later actively engaged in Jewish Renewal, including Rabbis Shefa Gold, Lynn Gottlieb and Waskow's partner Phyllis Berman. Initially the movement attracted little attention in the US Jewish community despite various articles in Jewish magazines. However, in 1973 Michael and Sharon Strassfeld published *The Jewish Catalogue: A Do-It-Yourself Kit*. This was patterned after the counter-culture *Whole Earth Catalogue* and served as a basic reference book dealing with a wide

*Above* Liberal political activist Rabbi Arthur Waskow (right), co-founder of the havurot movement and a leading figure in Jewish Renewal, with Muslim imam Mahdi Bray.

range of Jewish subjects, including traditional observances as well as crafts, recipes and meditational practices. In time the havurah movement increased in numbers and included self-governing havurot within Reform, Conservative and Reconstructionist congregations. By 1980 a number of havurot moved away from traditional patterns of Jewish worship as members added English readings, chants, poetry and other elements from various spiritual traditions.

## RENEWAL LEADERSHIP

Pre-eminent among leaders of this new movement was Zalman Schachter-Shalomi, a Hasidic-trained rabbi who was ordained in the Lubavitch movement. In the 1960s he broke with Orthodox Judaism and founded his own organization, the B'nai Or Religious Fellowship. The name 'B'nai Or' means 'sons' or 'children' of light, and was taken

*Left* Rabbi Zalman Schachter-Shalomi, with the Dalai Lama in Dharamsala, India, 1990. The rabbi is holding a chart explaining the similarities between Jewish and Tibetan views.

from the Dead Sea Scrolls where the sons of light battle with the sons of darkness.

Schachter-Shalomi viewed B'nai Or as a semi-monastic ashram community, based on various communal models of the 1960s and 70s. The community never materialized as he wished, yet it produced a number of important Renewal leaders. The *B'nai Or Newsletter* presented articles on Jewish mysticism, Hasidic stories and Schachter-Shalomi's philosophy, which was influenced by Buddhism and Sufism. Rabbi Zalman later held the Wisdom Chair at Naropa Institute, America's only Buddhist university.

After the first national Kallah conference in Radnor, Pennsylvania in 1985, the name B'nai Or was changed to P'nai Or (Faces of Light) to reflect the more egalitarian nature of Jewish Renewal. Together with Arthur Waskow, Schachter-Shalomi broadened the focus of the organization. In 1993 it merged with the Shalom Centre, founded by Rabbi Waskow to become ALEPH (Alliance for Jewish Renewal). This organization served as an overarching association for like-minded havurot.

However, some more Orthodox members of B'nai Or were not content with these changes and left the Renewal movement. This brought

*Right Wearing a prayer shawl and skullcap, a Jew practises yoga on the beach at Ashdod, Israel — an example of how Judaism is revitalised in contemporary life.*

about significant leadership changes, with Waskow taking an increasingly important role. During this period his magazine *Menorah* merged with the *B'nai Or Newsletter* to become *New Menorah*. This new publication addressed such issues as Jewish feminism, the nuclear arms race, new forms of prayer, social justice, and gay rights.

B'nai Or/ALEPH and its magazine led to the spread of Jewish Renewal throughout the United States and other countries. This has brought about the institutionalization of the movement in the form of the administrative ALEPH, the rabbinical association OHaLaH, and formalized rabbinic ordination programme.

## THE MOVEMENT

Statistical information about the number of Jews who affiliate with Jewish Renewal is not available. None the less, the movement has had a profound impact on various non-Orthodox streams of Judaism within the United States. Arguably the greatest impact has been on

Reconstructionist Judaism. Initially Reconstructionism was based on the rationalistic philosophy of Mordecai Kaplan, but, under the influence of Jewish Renewal, it has come to embrace Jewish mystical beliefs and practices, particularly in the prayer books that were issued in the 1990s.

Jewish Renewal has also had an impact on other non-Orthodox movements in terms of the increased leadership roles of women, the acceptance of gays and lesbians, and liberal political activism.

In addition, it is not uncommon for synagogues not associated with Jewish Renewal to feature workshops on Jewish meditation and yoga. Various melodies and liturgical innovations have been introduced through the influence of Renewal.

Despite such an impact on Jewish life, critics of Jewish Renewal maintain that the movement puts too much emphasis on individual spiritual experience over communal norms. Dismissed as a 'New Age' phenomenon, they argue that the borrowing from non-Jewish traditions has had a deleterious effect on Jewish life.

*Left Rabbi Zalman Schachter-Shalomi, perhaps Jewish Renewal's most prominent leader, in conversation with Tibetan Buddhist monks in Dharamsala, India, 1990.*

# MESSIANIC JUDAISM

AT THE CENTRE OF MESSIANIC JEWISH BELIEF AND PRACTICE IS THE CONVICTION THAT JESUS, WHO IS REFERRED TO AS YESHUA, IS THE LONG-AWAITED MESSIAH OR ANOINTED ONE.

Firmly rejected by the Jewish community as a whole, Messianic Judaism claims to be an authentic interpretation of the Jewish tradition. In the last few decades it has emerged as a controversial movement on the religious scene. Although followers see it as a legitimate interpretation of the tradition, this claim is firmly rejected by the Jewish community.

At the core of Messianic Jewish theology is the belief that Jesus (whom Messianic Jews refer to as Yeshua) is the long-awaited Messiah. Messianic believers contend that they are not Christians – rather they are determined to live Jewish lives in fulfilment of God's will. In this quest, Messianic Jews have reinterpreted the major Jewish festivals including Sabbath, Passover, Shavuot and Sukkot as well as festivals of joy and life-cycle events. At the centre of their practice and worship is the belief that the world has been redeemed and transformed.

*Below Rembrandt's* Head of Christ, *painted in 1748, shows the Christian Messiah as a Jewish man.*

## BIRTH OF A MOVEMENT

In the early 1970s a considerable number of American Jewish converts to Christianity (known as Hebrew Christians) were committed to a church-based conception of Hebrew Christianity. At the same time emerged a growing segment of the Hebrew Christian community seeking a more Jewish lifestyle. Particularly among the youth, there was a strong urge to identify with their Jewish roots. In their view, the acceptance of Yeshua should be coupled with a commitment to the cultural and religious features of the faith.

Eventually a clear division emerged between those who wished to forge a new lifestyle and those who sought to pursue traditional Hebrew Christian goals. The advocates of change sought to persuade older members of the need to embrace Jewish values, yet they remained unconvinced. In time the name of the movement was changed to Messianic Judaism – this brought about a fundamental shift in orientation. Any return to Hebrew Christianity was ruled out, and a significant number of older members left the movement.

## THEOLOGY

Messianic Judaism is grounded in the belief that Yeshua is the long-awaited Messiah. In this respect, Messianic Judaism and the earlier Hebrew Christian movement are based on the same belief system. None the less, Messianic Jews are anxious to point out there are important distinctions between their views and those of Hebrew Christians. Hebrew Christians see themselves as of Jewish origin and may desire to affirm their background, yet at the same time they

*Above Messianic Jews do not celebrate Mass but they mark festivals, such as the blessing of bread and wine on the Sabbath.*

view themselves as coming into the New Covenant. The Old Covenant has passed away. Hence, the direct practice of anything Jewish is contrary to their being part of the new people of God and the body of Christ. Messianic Jews, however, believe that the Jew is still called by God.

In the view of Messianic Jews, all of the prophecies in the *Tanakh* (Hebrew Bible) relating to messianic atonement were fulfilled in Yeshua. Repeatedly they affirm that the Messiah Yeshua came to the Jews, and his followers transmitted his message to the world. Although the Torah demands a blood sacrifice, the Messiah is able to offer himself as a means of atonement. Whereas traditional Judaism stresses that human effort is futile, what is required instead is belief in God's word and acceptance of the Messiah's atonement for sin. Only in this way can the faithful receive God's forgiveness and the promise of salvation.

Messianic Judaism asserts the world will be changed during the Second Coming. Drawing on the Suffering Servant passages in the Book of Isaiah, Messianic Jews argue that Yeshua fulfilled this role on earth but he will come again to deliver the world, defeat Israel's enemies, and establish God's Kingdom on earth.

*Above* Members of Sha'ar Adonai, a
Messianic congregation, dancing in
Central Park in New York.

*Right* A painting of Jesus, the Virgin
and the Child by Jewish master Marc
Chagall. The artist stresses the Jewishness of Jesus as the suffering Messiah.

## OBSERVANCE

Messianic Jews see themselves as the
true heirs of the early disciples of the
risen Lord. Anxious to identify with
the Jewish nation, Messianic Jews
have sought to observe the central
biblical festivals. In their view, the
Sabbath and the various festivals pre-
scribed in Scripture are as valid today
as they were in ancient times.

Customs regulating the life-cycle
and lifestyle of Jews in biblical times
are binding on members of the
Messianic community. Believers are
united in their loyalty to the Jewish
heritage as enshrined in Scripture.

None the less, Messianic Jews are
not legalistic in their approach to
Judaism. Traditional observance is
tempered with the desire to allow the
holy spirit to permeate the Messianic
community and animate believers in
their quest to serve the Lord. For this
reason, there is considerable freedom
among Messianic Jews in the ways
they incorporate the Jewish tradition into their daily lives.

*Right* Minister Jacques Elbaz preaches
to Messianic Jews in Tel Aviv, Israel.

The nature of contemporary
Messianic practice, means that
congregations do not rigidly follow
the patterns recommended in the
various Messianic prayer books produced by the movement; instead,
they modify their observance in
accordance with their own spiritual
needs. Visitors to Messianic congregations will thus be struck by the
considerable variation that exists
within the movement.

CHAPTER 4

# UNTRADITIONAL JUDAISM

Over the last two centuries, new interpretations of Jewish life have emerged. In the 1900s, Zionist thinkers argued a Jewish commonwealth must be established in the Holy Land. A few religious Zionists argued Jewry must actively bring about the creation of a Jewish presence in Palestine prior to the arrival of the Messiah. Secular Zionists maintained Jews would never be secure from anti-Semitism unless they had a nation state.

In recent years, other non-traditional movements have emerged in the Jewish community. Modern Kabbalists have tried to revitalize traditional Kabbalistic doctrines in the quest to live a more spiritual life. Jewish socialists have pressed for the restructuring of modern society. Jewish feminists have pressed for gender equality. Jewish Buddhists have reinterpeted Judaism. Jewish vegetarians espouse animal welfare. Other Jews advocate the acceptance of the pluralistic nature of modern Jewish life. Today Jews in Israel and the Diaspora follow a wide variety of different and conflicting paths in their quest to live an authentically Jewish existence.

*Opposite The years following the establishment of the State of Israel in 1948 saw the creation of many Jewish posters, such as this one from 1955 stressing environmental urban issues.*

***Above** Jewish women reach out to touch the Western Wall in Jerusalem, 2010. In modern times, Jewish feminists have re-evaluated the role of women in Jewish life.*

# RELIGIOUS ZIONISM

TRADITION IS THAT THE MESSIAH WILL LEAD THE JEWS BACK TO ZION.
IN CONTRAST, RELIGIOUS ZIONISTS ADVOCATED THE RETURN OF
JEWRY TO ISRAEL IN ANTICIPATION OF MESSIANIC DELIVERANCE.

For thousands of years Jews antici-pated that the coming of the Messiah would bring about a final ingather-ing of the Jewish people to their ancient homeland. This was to be a divinely predetermined miraculous event, which will inaugurate the messianic age. However, in the early 19th century within religious Orthodox circles there emerged a new trend, the advocacy of an active approach to Jewish messianism.

## THE STIRRINGS OF RELIGIOUS ZIONISM

At the beginning of the 19th cen-tury, a number of Jewish writers maintained that, rather than adopt a passive attitude towards the problem of redemption, the Jewish nation must engage in the creation of a homeland in anticipation of the advent of the Messiah. Pre-eminent

*Below* A Theological Debate *by Eduard Frankfort, 1888. By this date, the idea of a Jewish state was being fiercely debated among Orthodox Jews.*

among such religious Zionists was Yehuda hai Alkalai, born in 1798 in Sarajevo to Rabbi Sholomo Alkalai, the spiritual leader of the local Jewish community. During his youth, Yehuda lived in Palestine, where he was influenced by Kabbalistic thought. In 1825 he published a booklet enti-tled *Shema Yisrael* in which he advocated the establishment of Jewish colonies in Palestine, a view at vari-ance with the traditional Jewish belief that the Messiah will come through an act of divine deliverance.

When in 1840 the Jews of Damascus were charged with the blood libel (killing a child and using its blood in an act of ritual), Alkalai became convinced that the Jewish people could be secure only in their own land. Henceforth he published a series of books and pamphlets explaining his plan of self-redemp-tion. In *Minhat Yehuda* he argued on the basis of the Hebrew Scriptures that the Messiah will not miracu-lously materialize; rather, he will be preceded by various preparatory

*Above Abraham Isaac Kook, philosopher, mystic and defender of religious Zionism, who became the first Ashkenazi chief rabbi of Palestine before independence.*

events. In this light the Holy Land needs to be populated by Jewry in preparation for messianic deliver-ance. For Alkalai, redemption is not simply a divine affair – it is also a human concern requiring labour and persistence.

## THE GROWTH OF RELIGIOUS ZIONISM

Another early pioneer of religious Zionism was Zvi Hirsch Kalischer, the rabbi of Toun in the province of Posen, in Poland. An early defender of Orthodoxy against the advances made by Reform Judaism, he cham-pioned the commandments in prescribing faith in the Messiah and devotion to the Holy Land. In 1836 he expressed his commitment to Jewish settlement in Palestine in a letter to the head of the Berlin branch of the Rothschild family. The beginning of redemption, he main-tained, will come through natural causes by human effort to gather the scattered of Israel into the Holy Land. Later he published *Derishat Zion*. In this work he argued that the redemption of Israel will not take

place miraculously. Instead, it will occur slowly through awakening support from philanthropists and gaining the consent of other nations to the gathering of the Jewish people into the Holy Land.

Following in the footsteps of Alkalai and Kalischer, Abraham Isaac Kook formulated a vision of messianic redemption integrating the creation of a Jewish state. Born in Latvia in 1865, Kook received a traditional Jewish education and in 1895 became rabbi of Bausk. In 1904 he emigrated to Palestine, eventually becoming the first Ashkenazi chief rabbi after the British Mandate. Unlike secularists who advocated practical efforts to secure a Jewish state, Kook embarked on the task of reinterpreting the Jewish religious tradition to transform religious messianic anticipation into the basis for collaboration with the aspirations of modern Zionism.

## ORTHODOXY AND RELIGIOUS ZIONISM

Although some Orthodox Jewish figures endorsed the Zionist movement, Orthodoxy in Germany, Hungary and Eastern European countries protested against this new development in Jewish life.

To promote this policy, an ultra-Orthodox movement, Agudat Yisrael, was created to unite rabbis and laity against Zionism. Determined to counter Zionist ideology, Agudat denounced the policies of modern Zionists and refused to collaborate with religious Zionist parties such as the Mizrachi. In Palestine itself the extreme Orthodox movement joined with Agudat Israel in its struggle against Zionism.

Eventually, however, these critics of Zionist aspirations modified their position and began to take a more active role in Jewish settlement. This was owing to the immigration of members of Agudat Yisrael to Palestine, as well as the massacre of Orthodox Jews in Hebron, Safed and Jerusalem during the riots of 1929. None the less, the ultra-right refused to join the National Council of Palestinian Jewry, which had been established in the 1920s. In the next decades the rise of the Nazis and the events of the Holocaust brought about a split in the movement.

In 1934 Isaac Breuer, a leading Orthodox spokesman, cautioned that it would be a mistake to leave Jewish

*Left Hasidic Jew in Mea Shearim, home to ultra-Orthodox Jews in Jerusalem, 1985. Some Hasidic Jews oppose the idea of a Zionist state.*

*Above Entrance to a house in Mea Shearim, Jerusalem, a quarter outside the Old City walls, whose name means 'Hundred Gates'.*

history to the Zionists. If Agudat wished to gain the upper hand against the Zionists, it was obligated to prepare the Holy Land for the rule of God. In the unfolding of God's providential plan, he declared, the extreme Orthodox had a crucial role to play. Between the end of the war and the founding of the Jewish state, a zealous extreme group, the Neturei Karta in Jerusalem, accused the Agudat of succumbing to the Zionists. Yet, despite such criticism, the leaders of Agudat continued to support the creation of a Jewish homeland, and a year before its establishment they reached an understanding with Palestinian Zionists concerning such matters as Sabbath observance, dietary laws and regulations regarding education and marriage. Such a conciliatory policy paved the way for the creation of Orthodox religious parties in Israel, which continue to play a central role in the government of the Jewish state. Today, religious Zionists in Israel and the Diaspora regard the modern State of Israel as the fulfilment of God's promise to Abraham, Isaac and Jacob.

# SECULAR ZIONISM

IN THE 1880S AND 90S SECULAR ZIONISTS PROMOTED THE CREATION OF A JEWISH HOMELAND IN PALESTINE. IN THEIR VIEW, ONLY THE CREATION OF A JEWISH STATE WOULD PROTECT JEWS FROM THEIR ENEMIES.

The Russian pogroms of 1881–2 forced many Jews to emigrate to the United States, but a sizeable number were drawn to Palestine. These earlier pioneers were the vanguard of the Zionist movement, which agitated for the creation of a Jewish commonwealth in the Holy Land. In their view, anti-Semitism was inevitable; hence, they argued, Jewry could only be secure in a country of their own. This ideology was fuelled by an intense commitment to Jewish survival in a hostile world.

## ORIGINS
In the Russian Pale of Settlement, nationalist zealots organized Zionist groups (Lovers of Zion) which collected money and organized courses in Hebrew and Jewish history. In 1882 several thousand Jews left for Palestine, where they worked as shopkeepers and artisans; other

*Below* Portrait of Theodor Herzl, founder of political Zionism, painted in 1914 on the eve of World War I.

Jewish immigrants known as Bilu (from the Hebrew 'House of Jacob, let us go') combined Marxist ideals with Jewish nationalist fervour and worked as farmers and labourers.

During this period, Leo Pinsker, an eminent Russian physician, published *Autoemancipation* in which he argued that the liberation of Jewry could only be secured by the establishment of a Jewish homeland. 'Nations', he wrote, 'live side by side in a state of relative peace, which is based chiefly on fundamental equality between them. But it is different with the people of Israel. This people is not counted among the nations, because when it was exiled from its land it lost the essential attributes of nationality.'

## THE ZIONIST MOVEMENT
In the 1890s the idea of Jewish nationalism had spread to other countries in Europe. Foremost among its proponents was the Austrian journalist Theodor Herzl (1860–1904) who was profoundly influenced by the Dreyfus affair. In 1897, the first Zionist Congress took place in Basle, which called for a national home for Jews based on international law. At this congress Herzl stated that emancipation of the Jews had been an illusion. Jews were everywhere objects of contempt and hatred. The only solution to the Jewish problem, he argued, was the re-establishment of a Jewish homeland in Palestine.

In the same year the Zionist Organization was created with branches in Europe and America. After establishing these basic institutions of the Zionist movement, Herzl embarked on diplomatic

*Above* French editor Jean Jaurès, one of the most energetic defenders of Alfred Dreyfus. The Dreyfus affair persuaded Theodor Herzl of the necessity of a Jewish state to protect Jews.

negotiations. In 1898 he met with Kaiser Wilhelm II (ruled 1888–1918) who promised he would take up the matter with the Sultan. When nothing came of this, Herzl himself attempted to arrange an interview, and in 1901 a meeting with the Sultan took place. In return for a charter of Jewish settlement in Palestine, Herzl suggested that wealthy Jewish bankers might be willing to pay off the Turkish debt. In the following year the Sultan agreed to approve a plan of Jewish settlement throughout the Ottoman empire but not a corporate Jewish homeland in Palestine.

Unwilling to abandon a diplomatic approach, Herzl sought to cultivate contacts in England. In 1903 Joseph Chamberlain, the Secretary of State for Colonial Affairs, suggested the possibility of Uganda as a homeland for the Jews. At the next Zionist Congress in Basle this proposal was presented for ratification. When Chamberlain's scheme was explained, it was emphasized that Uganda was not meant to serve as a permanent solution but

*Above During an 1880s pogrom in Kiev, Russian Jews were assaulted while police did nothing. Such attacks convinced Zionists of the need for a Jewish state.*

rather as a temporary residence. When the resolution was passed by a small margin, delegates from eastern Europe walked out. Eventually the offer was withdrawn.

## EVOLUTION

After Herzl's death in 1904, David Wolffsohn became President of the Zionist movement. Under his leadership Orthodox Jews joined the Zionist Organization as members of the Mizrahi Party; socialist Jews also became members through the Labour Zionist Party. In the 1907 congress a resolution was passed which pledged the movement to the quest for a charter, the physical settlement of Palestine and the revival of the Hebrew language. During the next decade the major developments in the Zionist movement took place in Israel and by the beginning of the 20th century a sizeable number of Jews had migrated to Palestine.

Most of these pioneers lived in cities, but a small minority worked on farm colonies under the control of the Palestine Jewish Colonization Association. By 1929 the Jewish community in Palestine (*yishuv*) numbered 160,000 with 110 agricultural settlements; in the next ten years the community increased to 500,000 with 233 agricultural communities. During this time, rival Jewish factions emerged within Palestine with different political

*Above Arabs ready to attack Jewish buses from Jerusalem, 1948. As the Jewish population in Palestine increased, Zionists were constantly threatened by Arabs.*

orientations. The President of the World Zionist Congress, Chaim Weizmann (1874–1952), for example, was committed to co-operating with the British. Vladimir Jabotinsky (1880–1940), leader of the Union of Zionist Revisionists, stressed that the central aim of Zionism was the establishment of an independent state in the whole of Palestine.

## THE CREATION OF A JEWISH STATE

The Holocaust and the establishment of the State of Israel were organically related events: the death of millions of Jews in World War II profoundly affected Jewry throughout the world.

*Left David Ben-Gurion, the first Prime Minister of modern Israel, appointed two days after independence.*

During the war and afterwards, the British prevented illegal immigrants entering the Holy Land. In response, Jewish military forces joined together in resisting British policy. Eventually the British Government handed the problem of Palestine over to the United Nations. The UN discussed the Palestinian problem in May 1947. A special committee issued two reports; a minority recommended a federated bi-national state; the majority advocated a new plan of partition with a Jewish and Arab state as well as an international zone in Jerusalem.

This latter proposal was endorsed by the General Assembly of the United Nations on 29 November 1947. Once the UN plan of partition was endorsed, the Arabs began to attack Jewish settlements. By March 1948 more than thousand Jews had been killed, but in the next month David Ben-Gurion (1886–1973) ordered the Haganah to link up all the Jewish enclaves and consolidate the territory given to Israel under the UN partition plan.

On 14 May 1948 Ben-Gurion read out the Scroll of Independence in which he reiterated the goal of the Zionist movement: 'The Land of Israel was the birthplace of the Jewish people ... In the year 1897 the First Zionist Congress, inspired by Theodor Herzl's vision of the Jewish State, proclaimed the right of the Jewish people to national renewal in their own country.'

# MODERN KABBALISM

DRAWING ON ANCIENT KABBALISTIC TEACHING, MODERN KABBALISTS STRESS THE IMPORTANCE OF JEWISH MYSTICAL BELIEF AND PRACTICE. IN RECENT YEARS, THE KABBALAH CENTRE HAS ATTRACTED MILLIONS.

In contemporary society the Kabbalistic tradition has served as a rich spiritual resource for many Jews. In their quest to attain enlightenment, these religious seekers have embraced the teachings of modern Kabbalists. Pre-eminent among contemporary mystics Rav Philip Berg has drawn millions of Jews to the Kabbalistic tradition through the creation of Kabbalah Centres throughout the Jewish world.

## ORIGINS

The fundamentals of the medieval Kabbalistic system were expanded by such luminaries as Moses Cordovero, Isaac Luria, the Ba'al Shem Tov, Nachman of Bratslav, Levi Yitzhak of Berdichev, Kalonymus Kalman Epstein, Dov Baer of Mezhirich and Shneur Zalman. In

*Below The Chamsah, an amulet used to ward off the evil eye, from Safed, Israel, where Kabbalah developed.*

the modern period, interest in Kabbalistic thought outside the Hasidic circle generally diminished with the exception of such figures as Yehuda Ashlag, the author of *Sulam*, or 'Ladder', who influenced the development of popular Kabbalah. In recent years through his disciple Rav Berg, the international Kabbalah Centre has today become the most influential proponent of Kabbalistic thought worldwide.

Born in Warsaw in 1885, Ashlag was a descendent of scholars connected to the Hasidic courts of Prosov and Belz. In 1921 he moved to Palestine and worked as a labourer; later he was appointed rabbi of Givat Shaul, Jerusalem. In the 1930s he gathered around him a group of disciples who studied Kabbalah and promoted the study of Kabbalistic doctrine even for those who had not mastered rabbinic texts. In his view, knowledge of Kabbalah can provide all persons with a taste of Godliness that will enable them to conquer their evil inclinations and advance spiritually.

During this period Ashlag published *The Talmud of the Ten Sephirot*, which was a reworking of the thought of Isaac Luria; in addition he wrote an extensive commentary on the Zohar. In this work Ashlag stressed the transformation of human consciousness from a state of desiring to receive, to desiring to give. Through the study of Kabbalah, he believed, the mind opens to God's light, and the desire to give to others is developed. Ashlag believed that the coming of the Messiah meant that humans would give up their selfishness and devote themselves to loving each other.

*Above American rabbi Philip Berg of the Kabbalah Centre, which has had a powerful effect on Jews seeking inspiration from the Kabbalistic tradition.*

## THE KABBALAH CENTRE

Ashlag's main disciples included his sons Baruch Shalom and Shlomo Benyamin as well as Rabbi Yehuda Brandwein. Rabbi Baruch and Rabbi Brandwein influenced students who spread Ashlag's interpretation of Kabbalah. Brandwein's son-in-law Rabbi Avraham Sheinberger founded a commune in Israel, Or Ganuz, or 'The Hidden Light', which combines Ashlag's communal ideas with a devotion to Kabbalistic teaching.

In 1962 Rabbi Brandwein met Rav Philip Berg who had visited Israel from America. Trained in traditional yeshivot, Rav Berg was no longer a practising rabbi, but was deeply influenced by Rabbi Brandwein's teaching. In his autobiography, *Education of a Kabbalist*, Berg explained that he received the honour and responsibility of bringing the ancient wisdom of Kabbalah to the world.

As Brandwein's devoted student, Berg established the Kabbalah Research Centre, which today has 50 branches worldwide and has become the leading educational institution teaching the wisdom of the Kabbalah. Together with his sons Michael Berg and Yehuda Berg, Rav Berg has spread Kabbalistic teaching to millions of

*Above The return of Jewish mysticism is marked by a deepening interest in the way of Kabbalah.*

adherents. In a wide range of publications the Bergs have spread Ashlagian Kabbalism to disciples seeking spiritual knowledge and insight.

## KABBALISTIC THEOLOGY

Of central importance in the Kabbalistic system propounded by Rabbi Ashlag as explained by Rabbi Brandwein is the Desire to Share. This, he argued, should replace the Desire to Receive. According to Brandwein, human beings have been the gift of the desire to receive; this can be understood as an unusually large spiritual vessel containing the divine light. Yet it is a mixed blessing. Although it allows them to be persons to be filled with light, it can block them from true goodness. If individuals cannot transform their desire to receive into a Desire to Share, this will have the most negative results. The Desire to Receive will grow larger and larger until it swallows everything around it. Human history, Brandwein observed, is simply a record of self-serving desire run rampant, fuelled by hatred, envy and distrust.

Developing Brandwein's views, Rav Berg explains how spiritual growth is possible. Our souls, he asserted, are created for one reason only – the Creator in whom all things are invested, had a Desire to Share. But, when the Creator existed alone, sharing could not occur. There were no vessels to hold the endless bounty pouring out of him. So, with nothing more than desire, he created those vessels which are our souls. Initially these created souls received the divine light with no motive other than to receive for themselves alone. But as they were filled, a new yearning evolved – one that put them on a collision course with the Creator. Suddenly, in emulation of the Creator, our souls developed a Desire to Receive for the purpose of sharing. But they were faced with the same dilemma as that which faced the Creator himself before he created the vessels. With every soul filled, there was no one and nothing with whom to share.

Thus what Berg referred to as the 'Bread of Shame' came into being. This was shame at receiving so much and giving nothing in return. Shame at being in a position in which the soul had no opportunity to say yes or no to the Creator and, by that exercise of will, prove itself worthy to receive and thus dispel the shame. The shame led to rebellion – a mass rejection of the Creator's beneficence. When that happened, the light was withdrawn, darkness and the unclean worlds were created and all became finite – or limited – and thus in need of receiving. With those worlds came the clay bodies – vessels desiring only to receive for themselves alone – in which our souls reside. Here they forever struggle against body energy, to share. For the modern Kabbalist, this quest to eliminate the 'Bread of Shame' by sharing with others is the fundamental spiritual goal.

*Below Kabbalistic Jews mark the end of the Sabbath with Havdalah, reciting blessings over wine, a candle and spices.*

# THE JEWISH LEFT

IN THE LATE 19TH CENTURY SOCIALIST IDEALS INSPIRED A GROWING SEGMENT OF THE JEWISH COMMUNITY. CONTINUING THIS TRADITION, THE JEWISH LEFT PROMOTES SOCIAL ACTION IN MANY CONTEXTS.

The term Jewish Left refers to Jews who identify with or support left-wing causes either as individuals or through organizations. The Jewish Left is not a movement, yet those who support this political stance have been identified with various groups, including the US labour movement, the women's rights movement and anti-fascist organizations.

In contemporary society many well-known figures on the left have been Jews; these individuals were born into Jewish families and have in various ways been connected with the Jewish community, Jewish culture and the Jewish faith.

## ORIGINS

In the age of industrialization in the 19th century, a Jewish working class emerged in Eastern and Central Europe. Before long, a Jewish labour movement had emerged. The Jewish Labour Bund (or federation) was formed in Vilna in Lithuania in 1897. In addition, Jewish anarchist and socialist organizations were formed and spread across the Jewish Pale of Settlement in the Russian Empire. As Zionism grew in numbers, socialist Zionist parties were established. There were also non-Zionist left-wing forms of Jewish nationalism, such as territorialism (which advocated the creation of a Jewish national home but not necessarily in Palestine), autonomism (which supported non-territorial national rights for Jews in multinational empires), and folkism (which celebrated Jewish culture).

As Eastern European Jews emigrated in the 1880s, these ideological positions took root in various Jewish communities, particularly in England, New York and Buenos Aires. In the United States, the Jewish socialist movement embraced various organs including the Yiddish-language daily, the *Forward*, trade unions such as the International Ladies Garment Workers' Union, and the Amalgamated Clothing Workers.

***Above*** *Rose Pesotta, a Ukrainian Jew who came to the USA in 1917, became a feminist organizer and vice president of the International Ladies' Garment Workers' Union.*

In the late 19th and early 20th centuries, Jews played a major role in the Social Democratic parties in Germany, Russia, Austria–Hungary and Poland.

## STALINISM AND FASCISM

Many Jews worldwide welcomed the Russian Revolution of 1917, celebrating the eclipse of a regime which had fostered anti-Semitism. In their view, the new order in Russia would bring about the amelioration of Jewish life. A number of Jews joined the Communist party in Great Britain and the United States. As a result, there were Jewish sections of various Communist parties such as the Yevsektsiya in the Soviet Union. In the USSR the Communist regime adopted an ambivalent attitude

***Left*** *Many Jews welcomed the Russian Revolution. These members of the Jewish Society in St Petersburg are holding a banner in Yiddish that reads, 'Jewish Socialist Workers Party', 1918.*

*Above* Political theorist Hannah Arendt, *a German Jew, who reported for the* New Yorker *on the war crimes trial of the Nazi Adolf Eichmann.*

towards Jewry and Jewish civilization; at times it supported the development of a Jewish national culture, yet the party also carried out anti-Semitic purges. With the rise of fascism in Europe in the 1920s and 1930s, many Jews became involved in the left, particularly within Communist circles, which were fiercely opposed to

fascism. During World War II the Jewish left played a major role in the resistance to Nazism.

## THE LEFT IN CENTRAL AND WESTERN EUROPE

Alongside Jewish working-class movements, assimilated middle-class Jews in Central and Western Europe began to search for sources of radicalism in the Jewish tradition. Martin Buber, for example, was influenced by Hasidic texts in formulating his philosophy; Walter Benjamin was inspired by Marxism and Jewish messianism; Jacob Israel de Haan combined socialism with Orthodox Judaism; in Germany, Walther Rathenau was an important figure of the Jewish Left.

## SOCIALIST ZIONISM

In the 20th century, socialist Zionism became an increasingly important factor in Palestine. Poale Zion, or 'Workers of Zion', the Histadrut labour union and the Mapai party were important in Israel and included within their ranks such politicians as Israel's first and fourth prime ministers David Ben-Gurion and Golda Meir. At the same time, the kibbutz movement was grounded in socialist ideals.

In the 1940s many on the left advocated a bi-national state in Israel/Palestine rather than an exclusively Jewish state. This position was supported by such figures as Hannah Arendt and Martin Buber. Since Israeli independence in 1948, the left has been represented by the Labour Party, Meretz and the Palestine Communist Party, Maki. There are two worldwide left-wing Zionist organizations: namely the World Labour Zionist Movement and the World Zionist Organization.

*Left* This anti-Semitic cartoon of 1900 *alleges Jews were plotting to destablize Russia. Many Russian Zionists supported the creation of a Jewish homeland in Palestine.*

*Above* Israel's first and fourth prime *ministers Golda Meir and David Ben-Gurion at London Airport, 1961.*

## THE CONTEMPORARY LEFT

The Jewish working class died out following World War II, but there are still some survivals of the Jewish working class left, including the Jewish Labour Committee and *Forward* newspaper in New York, the Bund in Melbourne, Australia, and the Labour Friends of Israel in the UK.

Throughout the 1960s and 1970s there was a renewal of interest in the West in working-class culture and in various radical positions of the past. This interest led to the development of a new form of radical Jewish organizations that were interested in Yiddish culture, Jewish spirituality and social justice, such as the New Jewish Agenda, the Jewish Socialists' Group in Britain, and the magazine *Tikkun*.

In addition, there has been a strong Jewish presence in the anti-Zionist movement, including such figures as Norman Finkelstein and Noam Chomsky. In Israel, left-wing political parties and blocs continue to play a significant role in the Jewish state.

# JEWISH FEMINISM

INSPIRED BY THE FEMINIST MOVEMENT, JEWISH FEMINISM PROMOTES THE RIGHTS OF JEWISH WOMEN. CRITICAL OF MALE DOMINANCE IN RELIGIOUS LIFE, THEY WORK FOR AN EQUAL ROLE IN ALL SPHERES.

The Jewish feminist movement seeks to improve the status of women within Judaism and to open up new opportunities for religious experience and leadership. An offshoot of the feminist movement, it originated in the early 1970s in the United States and has had a profound influence on contemporary Jewish life.

### ORIGINS

Jewish feminism was spurred by a grassroots development that took place in the 1970s. In the previous decade, many Jewish women had participated in the second wave of American feminism. At this time most of these women did not link their feminism to their religious or their ethnic indentification. However, eventually some women whose Jewishness was central to their self-understanding applied feminist insights to their condition as American Jewish women. Faced with a male religious establishment,

*Below Jewish feminists. Politician Bella Abzug with writer Gloria Steinem and the Revd Jesse Jackson.*

these women envisaged a new form of Jewish life, one that would embrace women's concerns.

At this stage two important articles appeared which pioneered the evolution of American Jewish feminism. In the fall of 1970 Trude Weiss-Rosmarin criticized the liabilities of Jewish women in 'The Unfreedom of Jewish Women' which appeared in the *Jewish Spectator* which she edited. Several months later, Rachel Adler, an Orthodox Jew, published an indictment of the status of women in *Davka*, a counter-culture journal.

### THE DEVELOPMENT OF JEWISH FEMINISM

Following these publications, Jewish feminism became a public phenomenon. A small group of feminists, calling themselves Ezrat Nashim (women's help), associated with the New York Havurah, a counter-cultural fellowship and took the issue of equality of women to the 1972 convention of the Conservative Rabbinical Assembly. In meetings with rabbis and their wives, members of Ezrat

*Above Bertha Pappenheim, Austrian feminist and founder of the Jüdischer Frauenbund (League of Jewish Women) in 1904.*

Nashim called for a change in the status of Jewish women. In their view, women should have equal access with men in occupying public roles of status and honour in the Jewish community. The group focused on eliminating the subordination of women by equalizing their rights in marriage and divorce laws, the study of sacred texts, including women in the *minyan*, or 'quorum necessary for communal prayer', and providing

*Below French feminist writer Elisabeth Badinter is a Jew and author of* Mother Love: Myth and Reality *(1980).*

opportunities for women to assume positions of leadership in the synagogue as rabbis and cantors. In the same year, the Reform movement took a fundamental step in this direction by ordaining Sally Priesand as the first female Reform rabbi.

In the following year, secular and religious Jewish feminists under the auspices of the North American Jewish Students' Network convened a conference in New York City. The next year a short-lived Jewish feminist organization was founded at a similar Jewish feminist conference. As time passed, Jewish feminists brought their message to a wider audience through various publications. Activists from Ezrat Nashim and the North American Jewish Students' Network published an issue of *Responsa* magazine dedicated to Jewish feminist concerns. In 1976, an expanded version entitled *The Jewish Woman: New Perspectives* appeared. The same year a Jewish feminist magazine *Lilith* was published.

## RITUALS AND RABBIS
Through their efforts, Jewish feminists gained increasing support. Innovations, such as baby-naming ceremonies, feminist Passover seders and ritual celebrations of the New Moon were introduced into communal settings in the home or synagogue. These ceremonies were

aimed at the community rather than the individual; in this way, Jewish feminists aimed to enhance women's religious roles in Jewish life. The concept of egalitarianism evoked a positive response from many American Jews. In the Reform movement, the principle of equality between the sexes became a cardinal principle. Similarly, within the Reconstructionist movement women were granted equal status, and in 1974 Sandy Eisenberg Sasso was ordained as a rabbi. In time the Conservative movement also accepted

*Above Women of the Wall wear prayer shawls and tallit, ritual garments traditionally associated with men, at the Western Wall, Jerusalem, 2010.*

the principle of equality: Amy Eilberg became the first female Conservative rabbi in 1985, and women were welcomed into the Conservative cantorate in 1987.

## BLU GREENBERG AND JOFA
In support of feminist principles, Blu Greenberg founded the Jewish Orthodox Feminist Alliance (JOFA) in 1997 to advocate women's increased participation in modern Orthodoxy and to create a community for women and men dedicated to principles of equality. In its mission statement, JOFA declares: 'The mission of the Jewish Orthodox Feminist Alliance is to expand the spiritual, ritual, intellectual and political opportunities for women within the framework of halakha. We advocate meaningful participation and equality for women in family life, synagogues, houses of learning and Jewish communal organizations to the full extent possible within halakha.'

## ORTHODOX FEMINISM
Even though the Conservative movement led the way for Jewish feminism in the 1970s and 1980s, Jewish feminism was interpreted in different ways in the Orthodox community. In 1981 Blu Greenberg made a case for Orthodox feminism in *On Being a Jewish Feminist*. Alongside this work, a small number of Orthodox feminists established women's *tefilah*, or 'prayer', groups that respected halakhic restraints on the role of women in Jewish life.

Even though the Orthodox leadership deny feminist claims of the secondary status of women within traditional Judaism, Jewish feminism has had an important impact on American Orthodoxy. Girls are provided with a more comprehensive education in Orthodox schools, and Orthodoxy has embraced such rituals as celebrations of the birth of a daughter and bat mitzvah rites.

# GENDER ISSUES

WITHIN THE JEWISH WORLD THERE ARE A SUBSTANTIAL NUMBER OF
GAY AND LESBIAN JEWS. YET THE VARIOUS MOVEMENTS WITHIN JUDAISM
DIFFER IN THEIR VIEW OF HOMOSEXUALITY.

In the Western world, many states now legalize civil partnerships between people of the same sex. Orthodox Jews may condemn such unions, but some non-Orthodox communities adopt a more liberal attitude.

## TRADITIONAL JUDAISM AND HOMOSEXUALITY

In the Bible, homosexual conduct between men is more frequently mentioned and condemned than homosexual practices between women. There is no reference to a homosexual tendency, rather it is the act which is forbidden. Thus Leviticus 19:20 states: 'Thou shalt not lie with mankind, as with

*Below A mother and her lesbian partner with their newborn son and female rabbi, California, 2004, the first year that same-sex marriages were permitted in the US state.*

*Right Chabad Lubavitch Hasidim protesting at the annual gay pride parade in Tel Aviv, Israel.*

womankind, it is an abomination.' Again, Leviticus 20:13 declares: 'And if a man lie with mankind, as with womankind, both of them have committed abomination; they shall surely be put to death; their blood shall be upon them.'

In the 2nd century CE, a debate is recorded in the Mishnah in which Rabbi Judah forbids two unmarried men to sleep together in the same bed, while the sages permit it. According to the Talmud, the reason why the sages disagree with Rabbi Judah is that Jews are not suspected of engaging in homosexual practices. Although the code of Jewish law records the opinion of the sages, it states: 'But in these times, when there are many loose-livers about,

a man should avoid being alone with another male.' According to the rabbis, Gentiles too are commanded by the Torah to abstain from male homosexual acts.

The sources, however, are less clear about lesbianism. The *Sifra* (midrash on Scripture) comments on Leviticus 18:3 ('After the doings of the land of Egypt wherein ye dwelt shall ye not do; and after the doings of the land of Canaan,

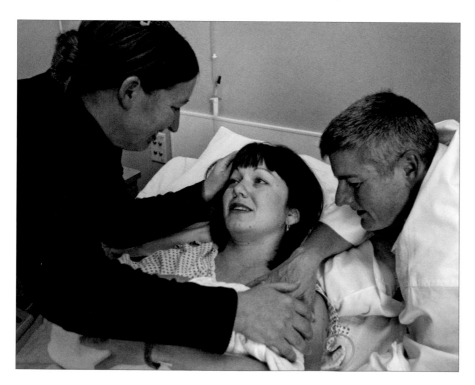

### WORLD CONGRESS
Today the movement for the acceptance of gay and lesbian Jews is a worldwide phenomenon. The World Congress of Gay, Lesbian, Bisexual and Transgender Jews, Keshet Ga'avah, consists of more than 25 member organizations. The Hebrew subtitle Keshet Ga'avah – Rainbow of Pride – emphasizes the importance of Hebrew and of Israel to the World Congress. Since its establishment in 1975, conferences have been held all over the world. Their vision is 'an environment where Lesbian, Gay, Bisexual and Transgender Jews worldwide can enjoy free and fulfilling lives.'

whither I bring you, shall ye not do; neither walk in their statutes.'), stating that what is being referred to are the sexual practices of the Egyptians and the Canaanites. The sin being referred to is marrying off a man to a man and a woman to a woman. The Talmud rules that women who perform sexual acts with one another should not be viewed as harlots, but as indulging in lewd practices.

According to the 12th-century Jewish philosopher and legalist Moses Maimonides, while lesbian practices are forbidden, a woman guilty of them should not be treated as an adulteress.

## CONSERVATIVE JUDAISM AND HOMOSEXUALITY

Despite such teaching, the more liberal branches of Judaism have in recent years embraced both gays and lesbians. Conservative Judaism did not allow for the ordination of openly gay men and women for over one hundred years. In addition, Conservative rabbis who performed same-sex commitment ceremonies did so without the Law Committee's sanction. Yet on 6 December 2006 the Committee on Jewish Law and Standards of the Rabbinical Assembly decreed that Conservative rabbis, synagogues and institutions can perform or host same-sex commitment ceremonies and are free to hire openly gay rabbis and cantors if they so wish. The decisions of the CJLS are only advisory, yet this body does represent the movement as a whole.

*Above A same-sex couple participating in a Jewish wedding ceremony at Beverly Hills, California, in 2008.*

## REFORM JUDAISM

More liberal in its outlook, the Reform movement actively supports the rights of gays and lesbians. Over the last two decades the Union of American Hebrew Congregations has admitted to membership several synagogues with an outreach to gay and lesbian Jews. Hundreds of men and women who previously felt alienated from Judaism have joined these synagogues and added their strength to the Jewish community.

In 1977 the Union of American Hebrew Congregations called for an end to discrimination against homosexuals, and in 1987 they expanded upon this by calling for inclusion of gay and lesbian Jews in all aspects of synagogue life. Subsequently the movement has embarked on a programme of heightened awareness and education to achieve the fuller acceptance of gay and lesbian Jews.

*Left Portrait of a gay Jewish couple marrying under the traditional* huppah *(a canopy with open sides) in Manhattan, New York.*

# JEWISH BUDDHISTS

JUBUS OR BUJUS SEEK TO BLEND THEIR JEWISH BACKGROUND WITH PRACTICES DRAWN FROM THE BUDDHIST TRADITION. THIS SPIRITUAL PATH OFFERS BELIEVERS A MEANS OF ENTRY INTO JUDAISM.

The members of the Jewish Buddhist movement (known as Jubus or Bujus) seek to combine their Jewish background with practices drawn from the Buddhist tradition. The term Jubu was first brought into circulation with the publication of *The Jew in the Lotus* by Rodger Kamenetz. The majority of Jewish Buddhists maintain their religious convictions and practices in Judaism coupled with Buddhist beliefs and observances.

The first instance of an American being converted to Buddhism in the USA occurred at the 1893 exposition on world religions. The convert, Charles Strauss, stated that he was a Buddhist at a public lecture that followed the World Conference on Religions in the same year. Strauss later became an author and an expositor of Buddhism in the West. After World War II there was an increasing interest in Buddhism among Jews associated with the Beat generation. At that time Zen Buddhism was the most widely known form of the Buddhist tradition.

In the 1960s more Jews became interested in Buddhist teachings; prominent teachers included Joseph Goldstein, Jack Kornfield and Sharon Salzberg who founded the Insight Meditation Society and learned vipassana meditation primarily through Thai teachers.

THE ATTRACTION OF JUDAISM
Jewish Buddhists report that the encounter between Jews and Buddhism leads to a journey into a deeper spirituality by blending

*Above An iconic image of a stone Buddha embedded in tree roots at Wat Mahathat temple, Ayutthaya, Thailand.*

various elements of both traditions. For Jubus the Buddhist tradition provides a means of entry into the religious treasures of their own faith. As many individual followers are keen to point out, both Judaism and Buddhism contain a number of common practices: they both emphasize acting ethically. Each is based on a body of teachings passed on for thousands of years. Each teaches respect for spiritual teachers. Both stress that actions have consequences, but that errors can be atoned for and purified. Neither Jubus nor Bujus proselytize, though both accept newcomers. Jews and Buddhists alike treat their texts and holy objects with veneration. And significantly, some of their mystical teachings are similar.

BRIDGING TRADITIONS
On the surface it appears that the beliefs and rituals of Judaism and Buddhism could not be more different. Yet, Jubus argue that an immersion into Buddhism can serve to help Jews to discover their Jewish roots. The Jewish history of persecution and displacement, for example, is echoed by the treatment of Tibetan Buddhists at the hands of the Chinese; both Moses and the

## THE JEW IN THE LOTUS

In October 1990, the Jewish poet Rodger Kamenetz journeyed to Dharamsala, India, with a small group of rabbis and other Jewish leaders. There they met the Dalai Lama, the leader of Tibetan Buddhism who had been exiled from Tibet by the Chinese regime.

The book that emerged from this expedition was *The Jew in the*

*Above Rodger Kamenetz's* The Jew in the Lotus.

*Lotus: A Poet's Rediscovery of Jewish Identity in Buddhist India* (1994). This volume explores Kamenetz's reflections on his own Jewishness and the attraction that Buddhism holds for a significant number of Jews whom he referred to as Jubus.

In this study, Kamenetz expounds an interpretation of Judaism that offers a new form of spirituality to Jews so they need not turn to Buddhism or anywhere else. Candidly he chronicles his own struggles with what it means to be Jewish. Without knowing why, he sensed it is not enough to be a secular Jew; rather, he insisted, life calls for a spirituality of some sort.

*Above* The Dalai Lama, the leader of Tibetan Buddhism, praying at the Western Wall in Jerusalem.

Buddha had life-changing experiences that caused them to flee the royal court: both wandered – Buddha as a yoga practitioner and Moses as a shepherd. There is also a similarity between the tree of knowledge in Genesis and the Bodhi tree under which the Buddha was first enlightened. Jubus further point out that both traditions encourage questioning and debate. Despite the icons and statues associated with Buddhism, both religions reject images and forms of the Ultimate, conceiving the Absolute to transcend all form and limitation. For some Jubus, the eight-fold path of Buddhism helps to focus their spiritual and moral life.

JUDAISM AND BUDDHISM
Critics of the Jewish–Buddhist movement are anxious to point out the differences between Judaism and Buddhism. The most conspicuous difference concerns belief in God. While Judaism is the foundation of monotheism, Buddhists do not espouse belief in a supernatural deity.

*Right* Singer Leonard Cohen was ordained as a Buddhist monk but says 'I'm not looking for a new religion. I'm quite happy with the old one, with Judaism.'

According to tradition, when the historical Buddha was asked whether or not God exists, he remained silent. This silence was interpreted in two ways: either he intended to demonstrate that God is beyond words, or that he considered theism as irrelevant to his doctrine. This latter approach has been widely accepted among Buddhists through the centuries.

The doctrine of no-self is also foreign to Jewish consciousness. According to Buddhist philosophy, the annihilation of the ego is conceived as seeing through the illusion of the historically conditioned self as a fixed entity. Even though Jewish

*Above* Rabbi David Saperstein, the Dalai Lama and Rodger Kamenetz at the Seder for Tibet, 1997, a concrete example of Jewish–Buddhist dialogue.

mysticism extols the transcendence of the ego, this path is not an end in itself. The Jewish mystic is obliged to continue to keep the mitzvot and to remain an individual member of a Jewish community. Selfhood is fundamental to the Jewish notion of obedience to the divine will. Yet, despite such observations, Jubus insist that they are living an authentic Jewish existence enlightened by insights from a rich tradition of spiritual resources.

# JEWS AND THE ENVIRONMENT

ALONGSIDE CONCERNS ABOUT ANIMAL WELFARE, MANY JEWISH PEOPLE TODAY ALSO FOCUS ON THE SIGNIFICANCE OF NUMEROUS ENVIRONMENTAL THREATS.

Acid rain, the greenhouse effect, ozone layer depletion, erosion of topsoil, destruction of forests and other habitats, pollution of water and soil, and toxic waste pose fundamental problems in the modern world. Given that Judaism teaches that the earth is the Lord's and that we are to be partners and co-workers with God in protecting the environment, Jews have ecological responsibilities towards the planet. Across the religious spectrum, a growing number of Jews embrace ecological principles rooted in the tradition.

## HUMAN RESPONSIBILITY FOR NATURE

In the 21st century, concern with the preservation of the planet has become of central importance. The proliferation of vast industries throughout the globe, the danger of

*Right An Ultra-Orthodox Jewish man showers after bathing in the Dead Sea, where Orthodox Jews have dedicated areas. Such rituals are linked to respect for the natural world.*

overpopulation, the risk of global warming – these and a range of other issues have contributed to anxiety about the ecological state of the world. In the past, these problems were not central to Judaism. On the contrary, Scripture asserts that human beings are to master the environment: 'And replenish the earth, and subdue it; and have dominion over the fish of the sea, and over the fowl of the air, and over every living thing that creepeth upon the earth' (Genesis 1:28). This does not mean, however, that in the older Jewish sources there was no concern with conservation. On the

contrary, human beings are to exercise care in dealing with nature. Human freedom to act should be in God's name and by his authority.

## CREATION & STEWARDSHIP

Genesis 1.31 declares that God found all of creation 'very good'. This implies that creation is sufficient, structured and harmonious. Scripture teaches that God has absolute ownership over creation. The environmental implications are that human beings are not to misuse nature. Everything belongs to God – as a consequence the use of the natural world must always be related to the larger good, and human concerns should not be elevated above everything else. Having been created in the image of God, humans are to have a special place and role. Of all of God's creatures, only they have the power to disrupt the natural world. This power comes from special characteristics that no other creature possesses. Humanity was placed on earth to act as God's agents and to actualize his presence as his stewards.

*Left Much of the Amazon rainforest has been destroyed in recent years. Jewish environmentalists seek to take responsibility for protecting the planet from such devastation.*

## LOVE AND AWE

As God's representatives on earth, humanity is connected to the rhythms of nature, the biogeochemical cycles, and the complex diversity of ecological systems. In Judaism, human responsibility growing out of such awareness is perceived as the fulfilment of the commandment to love and fear God. As the 12th-century Jewish philosopher Maimonides explained in the *Mishnah Torah*: 'When a person observes God's works and God's great and marvellous creatures, and they see from them God's wisdom that is without estimate or end, immediately they will love God, praise God and long with a great desire to know God's great name ... And when a person thinks about these things they draw back and are afraid and realizes that they are small lowly and obscure, endowed with slight and slender intelligence, standing in the presence of God who is perfect knowledge.'

## THE BIBLE AND THE ENVIRONMENT

A central text in understanding the Jewish concern for the environment concerns the prohibition of cutting down trees in a time of war. Deuteronomy 20:19–20 teaches: 'When in your war against a city you have to besiege it a long time in order to capture it, you must not destroy the trees wielding the axe against them. You may eat of them, but you must not cut them down. Are trees of the field human to withdraw before you into the besieged city? Only trees that you know do not yield field food may be destroyed; you may cut them down for constructing siegeworks against the city that is waging war on you, until it has been reduced.'

In rabbinic sources this law was expanded to include the prohibition of the wanton destruction of household goods, clothes, buildings,

springs, food and the wasteful consumption of anything. The underlying idea is the recognition that everything we own belongs to God. When we consume in a wasteful manner, we damage creation and violate the commandment to use creation only for legitimate ends. Restraint in consumption is hence a cardinal value within the tradition.

## THE SABBATH

Sabbath observance is one way to engender this sense of love and humility before creation. For one day out of seven, observant Jews limit their use of resources. Traditionally

*Above Since Israel's founding in 1948, agriculture and ecology has played an important part there. Poster of an Israeli farmer harvesting grapes, 1949.*

they do not do any work; the day is set aside for contemplation of the meaning of life.

Through Sabbath prayer the Jewish community is able to recognize that everything comes from God. Hence when Jews recite a blessing, they create a sacred pause in the flow of time to contemplate their place in the universe. At this moment they can see the world as an object of divine concern and place themselves beyond selfish desire.

# JEWISH VEGETARIANISM

IN THE MODERN WORLD, A GROWING NUMBER OF JEWS FROM ACROSS THE RELIGIOUS SPECTRUM HAVE EMBRACED VEGETARIANISM AS AN AUTHENTIC MODE OF JEWISH LIVING.

Many people see Jewish vegetarianism as both a philosophy and a life style based on Jewish theology.

## THE BIBLICAL BACKGROUND

According to Rabbi Abraham Isaac Kook (1865–1935), the first chief rabbi of Israel, vegetarianism is the ideal, symbolizing the ultimate peace between human beings and the animal kingdom. In his view, in the Messianic Age as prophesied in the Book of Isaiah, everyone will adopt a vegetarian diet. The only sacrifices that will be offered in the Temple will be the minhah sacrifice, which is of vegetable origin. Even though

*Below Jewish rug depicting Adam and Eve, made in Turkey, late 19th century. According to tradition, humans were vegetarian until the time of the Flood.*

there has been some debate regarding Kook's consistency in following a vegetarian diet, Rabbi She'ar Yashuv Cohen, the Chief Rabbi of Haifa, declared: 'I am a vegetarian, following in the footsteps of my late father, Rabbi David Cohen, and his teacher, the saintly first Chief Rabbi of Israel, Abraham Isaac Kook.'

According to Jewish vegetarians, in the ideal state of Gan Eden (the Garden of Eden) humans were described as vegetarian, and this state of affairs continued until after the Great Flood in the time of Noah. Other prominent figures who have followed a vegetarian lifestyle based on such biblical ideas include Rabbi David Rosen, former Chief Rabbi of Ireland, the late Rabbi Shlomo Goren, Chief Rabbi of Israel, and Avraham Burg, an elected Knesset Speaker.

*Above Abraham Isaac Kook, 20th-century philosopher, who promoted vegetarianism as a Jewish ideal.*

## ETHICAL PRINCIPLES

Judaism forbids the infliction of unnecessary pain and suffering. The principle of *tsaar baalei hayyim*, or 'preventing the suffering of living creatures', is extolled in biblical and rabbinic sources. Although this principle is not explicitly formulated in Scripture, it is based on biblical teaching concerning the compassionate treatment of God's creatures. Such an attitude shows an early appreciation of the sentiency of other creatures, and according to the rabbis, Israel was unique among the nations in advocating this approach.

On this assumption, rabbinic codes of law enshrine the principle of tsaar baalei hayyim as an important feature of the faith. Specifically, the rabbis continued to legislate concerning Sabbaths and festivals. For example, rabbinic legislation stipulates that animals – like human beings – should be allowed to move about wearing bandages and splints for their wounds, and that cushions should be supplied if needed.

Further, one is allowed to put salve and oil on an animal's wound and seek assistance of a gentile if milking is required. Again, it is

allowed to put an animal in cold water so as to cool it off as a remedy for congestion, or raise it out of a body of water into which it has fallen. It is also permitted to relieve a burden from an animal if it is in pain. Given the centrality of this concept of tsaar baalei hayyim, Jewish vegetarians maintain that their life style is the ideal ethical option, one that more clearly approximates to the original will of the creator.

## HEALTH CONCERNS

Recently a number of medical scientists have stressed that a plant-based diet is more healthy than a diet which includes meat. The Jewish tradition emphasizes the importance of maintaining health. Hence Jews are commanded in Deuteronomy 4:15: 'You shall guard yourselves most diligently.' This implies that everything possible must be done to protect health and avoid unnecessary risks. Further, Jews are obliged to 'choose life above all'. (Deuteronomy 30:19). The Talmud states that a danger to health takes precedence over ritual obligations. The Torah also declares that preven-

tion is the highest form of health. In this light, Jewish vegetarians maintain that they are following both biblical and rabbinic principles in adopting a vegetarian lifestyle.

In this regard, Jewish vegetarians point out that elevated blood cholesterol levels, high blood pressure and diabetes, all of which contribute to heart disease, can be alleviated by a high fibre, low-fat vegetarian diet coupled with a vigorous regime of exercise and stress reduction.

Similarly, the risk of lung cancer may be increased by animal-fat consumption. Meat consumption is a major risk factor for prostate cancer. Breast cancer may be linked with higher oestrogen levels and may reflect childhood dietary practices. Cancer of the colon is strongly linked to red and white meat consumption. Further, meat consumption is a risk factor for pancreatic cancer. Ovarian cancer has also been linked with dairy, egg and meat consumption.

*Left Jewish writer and Nobel Prize winner Isaac Bashevis Singer eating a vegetarian lunch in his apartment in Miami Beach, Florida, 1981.*

*Above The deforestation of the Amazon in recent years is an issue important to Jews concerned with the conservation of our planet.*

Further, lymphoma has been linked with beef and dairy consumption. Finally, the risk of bladder cancer in non-vegetarians is twice that of vegetarians.

## ECOLOGICAL CONCERNS

As an extension of the concern with animal welfare, many Jewish vegetarians also focus on the significance of numerous environmental threats. Acid rain, the greenhouse effect, ozone layer depletion, erosion of topsoil, destruction of forests and other habitats, pollution of water and soil, and toxic waste pose fundamental problems in the modern world.

Given that Judaism teaches that the earth is the Lord's and that we are to be partners and co-workers with God in protecting the environment, Jews have ecological responsibilities towards the planet. Hence, it is vital that Jewish values be applied in the solution of these pressing problems.

# INDEX

*Below Sabbath wine.*